FOOD AND CLOTHING

HISTORY OF INVENTION

FOOD AND CLOTHING

Daniel Gilpin

Facts On File, Inc.

Facts On File, Inc.
132 West 31st Street
New York, NY 10001

Library of Congress Cataloging-in-Publication Data

Gilpin, Daniel
   Food and Clothing / Daniel Gilpin
      p. cm.
   Summary: Outlines the development of what we eat and wear today, from primitive hunting and gathering to genetically engineered food, and from animal skins to spandex.
   Includes bibliographical references and index.
   ISBN 0-8160-5441-X
   1. Food habits—Juvenile literature. 2. Agriculture—Juvenile literature. 3. Hunting—Juvenile literature. 4. Clothing and dress—Juvenile literature. [1. Food habits—History. 2. Agriculture—History. 3. Hunting—History. 4. Clothing and dress—History.] I. Title.

GT2850.G54 2004
394.1/2 22—pcc lcac

2003047294

Facts On File books are available at special discounts when purchased in bulk quantities for businesses, associations, institutions, or sales promotions. Please call our Special Sales Department in New York at (212) 967-8800 or (800) 322-8755.

You can find Facts On File on the World Wide Web at
http://www.factsonfile.com

For The Brown Reference Group plc:
Project Editor: Tom Jackson
Design: Bradbury and Williams
Picture Research: Becky Cox
Managing Editor: Bridget Giles
Consultant: Dr. Martyn D. Wheeler, University of
   Leicester, United Kingdom.

Printed and bound in Singapore

10 9 8 7 6 5 4 3 2 1

CONTENTS

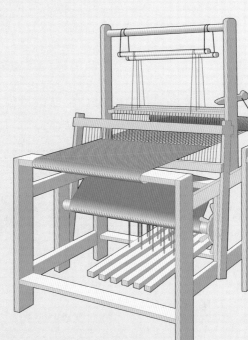

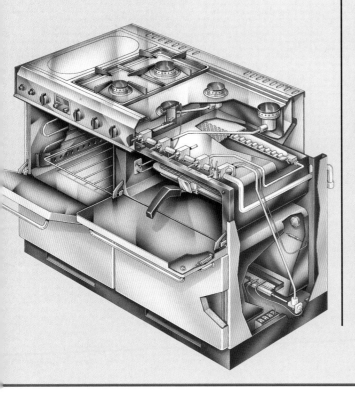

HUNTING AND GATHERING

sharp edge | handle

**Before people
farmed, they lived**
on what they were able
to take from the wild. They
gathered fruits, nuts, and tubers
and added to their diet with
hunted meat. This hunter-gatherer
lifestyle of our ancient ancestors
stretches back at least two million
years, and probably many millions
more. Growing food, by contrast,
is a relatively recent development.
Agriculture can be traced back
less than 20,000 years.

The first hunter-gatherers were
like us in most respects, but they
were not identical to modern
humans. They belonged to the
species *Homo erectus*, thought by
most scientists to be the direct
ancestor of our species, *Homo
sapiens*. *Homo erectus* evolved in
Africa. They hunted there with
simple clubs and sticks, not

specially designed weapons,
although they used simple tools.
Homo erectus probably chased
prey until it dropped from
exhaustion then killed it with
rocks and sticks.

Dead animals were butchered
using hand axes. These primitive
but effective tools were fashioned
from flint stones. When chipped,
flint fractures like glass. Very
sharp cutting edges can be made.

Outside Africa, *Homo erectus*
developed other tools. Some
scientists think that *Homo erectus*
may have used the tough, straight
stems of the bamboo plant to
make staffs and spears in Asia
1.8 million years ago.

*A hand axe made
by someone chipping
sharp edges into
the sides of a flint
stone. The other
end is kept blunt
and used as
a handle.*

MODERN HUMANS

Our own species, *Homo sapiens*, is around 150,000 years old. These people looked physically identical to us. Their brains were the same size as ours, suggesting that they could think as much and as well as we do. They were modern humans.

Like the ancestral *Homo erectus*, *Homo sapiens* evolved in Africa and spread to other parts of the world. Modern humans arrived in the Middle East and much of Asia about 90,000 years ago. By 50,000 years ago they had reached Australia, and 10,000 years later they began to appear in Europe. Finally, 12,000 years ago, *Homo sapiens* arrived in the Americas. The colonization of the world by modern humans was all but complete. People spread around the world so rapidly because of important developments in technology.

With their big brains and nimble fingers, modern humans were quick to improve on the tools used by their ancestors. Stone-working was refined and new hunting weapons invented. By 70,000 years ago, people in Africa had begun making microliths. These flaked stones were too small to have been used by hand. Microliths were set into wood to make other tools. Leaf-shaped blades were used for spear tips, and straight-edged ones for making knives. Other inventions made gathering easier, such as sacks sewn from animal skins.

wooden handle

stone head

The head is tied to the handle with sinew.

People improved tool technology by using new materials. The wooden handle on this axe increases its power and accuracy greatly when compared with a hand axe.

7

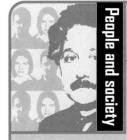

Modern-Day Hunters and Gatherers

In parts of Africa and Asia a few groups of people still hunt or gather a lot of their food. Perhaps among the most famous are the San, whose homeland is the Kalahari Desert. The often green, but always dry, Kalahari covers almost all of Botswana, the eastern third of Namibia, and the northernmost part of southwest South Africa. The San people are sometimes called "bushmen" but many consider this an insulting term. Even *San* is a name used by outsiders to refer to what are several groups who speak different (but related) languages, not a single ethnic group. Until the early 1900s, San people hunted or gathered most of their food. For that reason, they are sometimes called "Stone Age Peoples" and considered to be living reminders of humanity's prehistoric hunting-gathering lifestyles. It is impossible to know whether or not San society and culture, which has evolved over thousands of years to suit a particular landscape, compares to that of early Stone Age peoples who lived millions of years ago. There are sure to be many differences as well.

In the past, San people lived and traveled in close-knit groups, ranging from small family units to bands of 80 or more. Groups had no chiefs and shared food equally. Food-finding duties were divided between the sexes. San women were gatherers and collected grubs, roots, fruits, and seeds. San men were hunters and provided meat for the group. The bulk of the food was gathered not hunted, but meat provided vital protein and energy-rich fats. The men hunted using bows and arrows (below); the women dug for roots with sharpened sticks. A San hunt was often long and exhausting, a test of endurance as well as skill. Prey was tracked and chased until it dropped from thirst and exhaustion. In the hot, dry Kalahari the hunters could keep going for longer than their prey because they carried water.

Today, few San speakers live solely from hunting and gathering. Many now work for cattle herders and ranchers. Most San people have been resettled by the government of Botswana from their homes in the Central Kalahari Game Reserve to new villages outside the reserve. Only a few groups still hunt and gather for substantial portions of their livelihood. Even these groups add to their diet with farmed grains and tend herds of cattle, goats, and sheep. Whether settled or not, many San people engrave ostrich eggshells to sell to the tourist market. Such trade might have gone on for hundreds of years, since San people have long made water flasks from ostrich eggs.

The San have a rich cultural heritage and a detailed understanding of nature. Women and men can be powerful healers whom non-San people travel miles to consult. Healers use local plant remedies and religious rituals. The San's knowledge of native plants has led drug companies to a new discovery. Extracts from the *hoodia* plant, chewed by the San to suppress hunger, are being used in a new slimming pill. The San people are set to benefit financially from this drug. After a legal battle fought on their behalf, the San have been guaranteed a share of the royalties earned from any future sales of the drug.

Fur Trapping

Hunting provided prehistoric people with more than just food. It also gave them a ready supply of skins for clothing. Few people in North America hunt for food. Yet many still make a living from trapping animals for their fur.

Fur trapping has a long history in the more northerly parts of the world. The technology involved has changed little over the years. People have used snares since prehistory. These noose-like loops pull tight around an animal's head or legs. Snares are still used by many trappers today. Spring-loaded foothold traps are a more modern invention. Foothold traps have two fearsome metal jaws held open with a trip mechanism located beneath a metal plate. When an animal steps on the plate, the jaws snap shut. The jaws hold the animal until the trapper returns. So-called humane traps hold the animal without cutting into the flesh as much.

People now use less fur in clothing, but trapping remains big business. There are probably close to half a million active fur trappers in the United States. Half that number are employed in fur processing, marketing, and clothes manufacture.

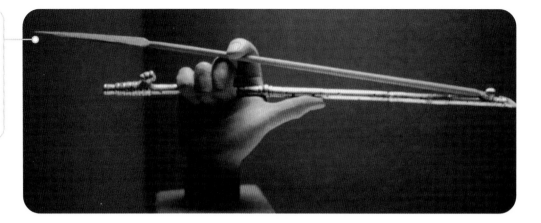

A gold atlatl, or spear thrower, from South America. This tool increased the range and power of a hunter's throw.

Aboriginal peoples in Australia use boomerangs, a range of wooden hunting tools that skilled hunters throw far and fast. The type below is designed to travel in a curve back to the thrower.

NEW TOOLS AND WEAPONS

As people developed better weapons, the range of animals they could hunt grew larger. People discovered that they could carve bone and antler to make weapons that lasted beyond one use. Simple spearheads were adapted to catch new types of prey. By adding backward-pointing barbs, people could spear fish with less risk of them escaping. Later, people attached bone hooks to lines and caught fish that way.

One of the most significant developments in hunting was the invention of the bow and arrow. Rock paintings from the Sahara desert show that people have been using bows and arrows for at least 30,000 years. The bow and arrow not only made hunting easier but also made it safer. People could now kill animals from a distance without needing to chase them down and kill them at close range.

Prehistoric peoples developed different long-range weapons in various parts of the world, among them the boomerang, blowpipe, and slingshot. An invention that traveled the globe was the *atlatl*, or spear thrower. It appeared first in Africa. The atlatl was a wood or bone rod with a hook that fitted into a socket at the end of the spear shaft. The atlatl increased the power of a spear. The spear not only flew farther but also inflicted greater damage when it hit the target.

BISON HUNTERS

Native Americans ride through a stampeding herd of bison. The guns and horses introduced by Europeans made it much easier and safer to hunt these large beasts.

Probably the most famous subsistence hunters of recent centuries were the native peoples of North America's Great Plains. Groups such as the Kiowa, Blackfoot, and Sioux survived almost entirely by hunting. They did so by hunting just one main target animal, the American bison, or buffalo.

Before European explorers arrived, North America's bison numbered in the tens of millions. Vast herds migrated northward in the spring to feed on the lush new grass and give birth. The herds headed south again to avoid the northern winter.

The people of the plains hunted bison in a variety of ways. Before horses and guns were introduced to the continent people hunted bison on foot. The earliest Plains people used spears to kill the animals. Bows and arrows were introduced later.

Hunting bison on foot was a risky business. People lessened the danger by hunting in groups. They crept up on the herd to select an animal to hunt before attacking together. Signals coordinated the attack and ensured that each hunter knew which animal was to be killed. Some Plains people wore disguises, such as bison robes or wolf skins, to help them get within striking distance. (Bison stand their ground against an individual wolf and run only if wolves attack in numbers.)

Wherever possible, Native Americans used the landscape to their advantage when hunting. Rivers or deep snow slowed the bison and made

12

them easier to kill. In some places hunters used natural features to spectacular effect. Bison were stampeded over cliffs at traditional buffalo jumps. Runners or chasers guided the herd toward the cliff, where other people waited behind rocks or trees. When the bison appeared, the people came out of hiding, shouting and waving blankets to frighten the bison over the precipice. More people waited

When bison were common many Native American groups, such as this band of Arapaho people, lived a nomadic lifestyle, following herds across the prairie and sheltering in tentlike tepees.

near the foot of the cliff to slaughter the crippled animals after they fell.

The buffalo pound was another relatively safe method for killing bison in large numbers. One hunter dressed in a bison skin led the herd into a ravine. Other people lining the ravine stampeded the herd into a log corral and killed the animals with spears.

The arrival of horses in North America brought a new element to the bison hunt. Horses were first shipped from Europe by the Spanish early in the 1500s. The animals soon became an integral part of Native American culture. The Plains peoples used them to hunt bison on the move,

riding alongside their quarry before shooting them with a bow and arrow or gun.

The horse and the gun spelled the end for the huge bison herds. European settlers killed the beasts on an industrial scale for the highly prized meat and hides. Native Americans also slaughtered the animals in increased numbers, moving from purely subsistence hunting to selling surplus skins to traders.

By 1891 the total population of bison in the United States had been reduced to fewer than 1,000 animals. A way of life that had served the Plains peoples for thousands of years was effectively extinct.

Bison meat is hung out to dry into jerky.

A hunting lodge or tepee made from bison hide.

FARMING TAKES HOLD

Rice paddies are farmed in terraces in Indonesia. Terraces are steps cut into hillsides, making it possible to use steep land for growing crops.

In the middle of the last ice age, about 20,000 years ago and before people first reached the Americas, events were taking place in Egypt that would change the world. People who had previously lived on the move were beginning to settle into permanent homes. They planted grasses near to where they settled, and this became their main food supply. Those early Egyptian settlers were the first farmers. The grasses they planted were the ancestors of wheat.

These events were repeated around the world as different peoples learned to farm throughout history.

Egypt during the Ice Age was perfect for farming. The weather was much cooler then than it is in Egypt now but not so cold that frosts were a problem. Conditions were ideal for plant growth, especially in the fertile Nile River Valley. The river flooded annually, washing nutrient-rich silt over the land.

Wild Grasses

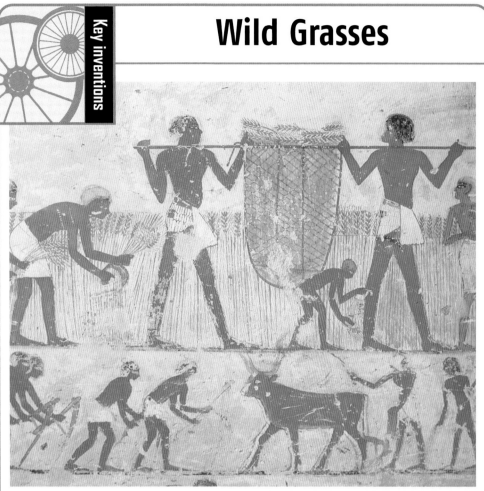

Strange though it may seem, grasses make up a large proportion of the food we eat today. Rice, wheat, and barley are all farmed forms of grasses. Foods as diverse as breakfast cereals, cakes, and bread all have grasses as their basic ingredients. The grasses grown as crops are very different from wild grasses. Farmed grasses have been bred over centuries for the size and nutrient content of their seeds, or grains. Some varieties are now genetically engineered in laboratories.

All of these crops are descended from wild ancestors. Wheat was probably the first crop. The earliest known wheat grains come from Egypt (above, in wall art) and are dated as 18,000 years old. Almost 20,000 cultivated varieties of bread wheat exist today. These can be traced back to three likely ancestors, all closely related to each other: einkorn (*Triticum monococcum*), emmer (*T. turgidum*), and a third species with no common name, *Triticum tauschii*.

Rice was first domesticated in the Indian region several thousand years ago. Its single wild ancestor, brownbeard rice (*Oryza rufipogon*), is a common plant throughout Asia. People have taken it to many other parts of the world.

Barley is almost as old as wheat. The earliest known cultivated barley grains were dug up in the area of modern-day Iraq and are 17,000 years old. Barley's wild ancestor, *Hordeum spontaneum*, still grows in the region.

ANIMAL HUSBANDRY

Soon after the Egyptians started planting crops the practice took hold in what is now Iraq. Like Egypt, this area was fed by life-giving river water. People grew barley here and later they were the first to raise domesticated animals. These tame animals rely on farmers for their food. They spend their entire lives on a farm. The animals are slaughtered for meat before they reach an old age. Wild sheep, or mouflon, were captured as lambs and raised by herders 10,000 years ago. Goats were domesticated from the bezoar ibex, a wild goat native to the area between the rivers.

As the centuries passed more and more plants and animals were domesticated. Dogs were kept for hunting or protection but most animals were raised for food, including milk as well as meat. By 5,000 years ago people were keeping pigs. These were wild boars raised from captured piglets. Domestic pigs emerged after years of breeding. The wild ancestor of cattle was called the auroch. This animal roamed through the forests of Europe in herds but is now extinct. Aurochs were domesticated 4,000 years ago. The first humped cattle were domesticated in Asia at around the same time. Their ancestor is the kouprey, which still lives in Cambodia and Laos.

At first few domestic animals except pigs were kept enclosed. People in medieval Europe, for example, grazed their livestock on publicly owned land.

An engraving depicting prehistoric Europeans hunting auroch, a wild ancestor of domestic cattle. Rearing domestic animals proved more reliable and less dangerous than hunting wild animals.

Domestic Breeding

Virtually every type of plant or animal farmed today is the result of domestic breeding. Domesticated varieties look different from their wild ancestors, such as the mouflon (above), because people bred them selectively for particular physical traits. Farmers mated sheep with the longest and thickest coats to breed the best wool-producing animals. Generations of selective breeding molded the breeds of sheep we see today. Cattle were bred for their milk yield or meat quality.

Domestic breeding was refined in the 18th century. but the mechanism behind it would not be understood fully for another 200 years. The results were obvious but no one could explain why two animals mated together produced the young that they did. That changed in the 1860s when an Austrian monk called Gregor Mendel started experimenting with garden peas. He bred peas plants with different seeds, flowers, and body sizes. Mendel found that the characteristics did not blend together in the next generation. Instead, one form tended to dominate over another. However, when he bred the resulting generation of crosses together, the seemingly lost characters reappeared. This revelation enabled people to develop more subtle methods of selective breeding. Mendel published his results in 1886 but the biologists of the time did not understand their significance fully. In 1901, other biologists performing similar research discovered Mendel did the work years before. Mendel's experiments became the basis of the modern science of genetics.

FARMING AROUND THE WORLD

Agriculture began in the Middle East but has long been practiced in many other parts of the world. In Asia, the staple crop has always been rice. Rice grows best with its roots in water. A unique method of cultivation developed around the rice plant.

Rice paddies or paddy fields are shallow ponds bordered by earthen dams. They are kept wet by water channelled from rivers and streams. Paddies often cover huge areas. In many parts of Asia hillsides are terraced to make more room for paddies. People use plows towed by water buffalo to tend the paddies. The water buffalo is the continent's main beast of burden and well suited to standing in water.

People in the Americas had their own methods of agriculture and raised their own crops. The Incas of Peru grew potatoes, tomatoes, and peppers. These plants have since become popular worldwide. Incas also farmed squashes and a wide range of other plants, as did the Aztecs and Maya of Central America. In North America farming was less developed. Most Native American tribes were hunter-gatherers. Some, such as the Iroquois, grew tobacco and corn.

Throughout the Americas, livestock was almost unknown. The Incas raised guinea pigs and ducks for the table. Alpacas were bred for their wool, and llamas kept as beasts of burden.

Our Best Friend

Dogs and people have lived together for at least 10,000 years. All dogs are descended from the gray wolf. The first dogs were wolves raised by people. Wolf cubs were probably taken from the wild and brought into human homes and settlements. There, they grew up recognizing people as their pack members and defended them and their territory accordingly. Over the centuries domesticated wolves were bred for characteristics such as loyalty, strength, or speed.

Slowly, animals that would be recognized as dogs rather than wolves began to appear. Some of these dogs were kept to protect other domesticated animals from wild predators, including wolves. Others were bred for hunting or tracking down game. A few were kept for food or even transport. There are more than 180 officially recognized dog breeds. They range in size from the mastiff, which may weigh significantly more than an adult person, to the Yorkshire terrier, which at its smallest may be no bigger than a large rat. Most dogs are now kept just as pets. Some, such as the Canadian Eskimo dog, or husky, continue to work for a living.

CROP PROTECTION

Just as early pastoral farmers' flocks and herds were at risk from predatory wild animals, so arable farmers suffered losses from creatures that ate their crops. Children frightened birds by ringing bells, blowing whistles, shouting, or shaking clappers and rattles. In the 18th century, European farmers started to use scarecrows to keep birds off crops. There was little that people could do about mice and insects.

The Plow

Key inventions

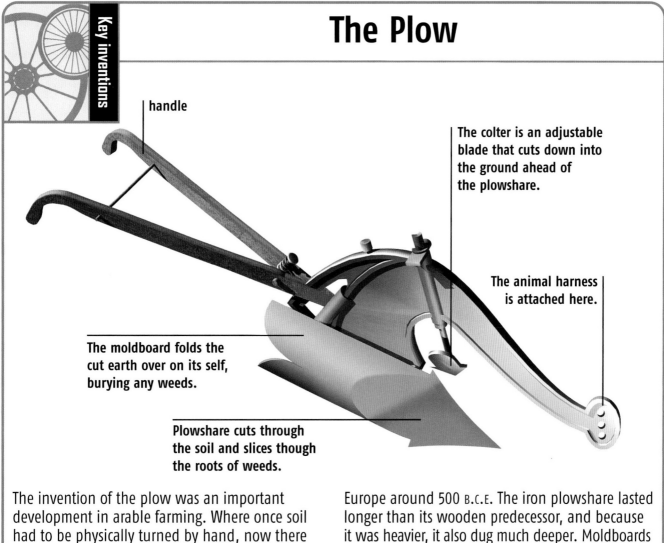

handle

The colter is an adjustable blade that cuts down into the ground ahead of the plowshare.

The animal harness is attached here.

The moldboard folds the cut earth over on its self, burying any weeds.

Plowshare cuts through the soil and slices though the roots of weeds.

The invention of the plow was an important development in arable farming. Where once soil had to be physically turned by hand, now there was a device that could speed the process up many times over. Plowing is important because it breaks up the soil, allowing in the air and water that plants need to grow. Turning the soil also buries weeds growing on the surface. The first plows appeared in Mesopotamia (modern Iraq) around 3500 B.C.E. These simple weighted sticks attached to oxen made it easier for farmers to break up the soil and make furrows for planting their seeds. The first iron plowshares appeared in Europe around 500 B.C.E. The iron plowshare lasted longer than its wooden predecessor, and because it was heavier, it also dug much deeper. Moldboards for turning the soil over and wheels were added to plows between the 7th and 10th centuries. The design then changed little for 800 years. In 1760, a new type of plow went into production at Rotherham, England. Based on a triangular frame it was stronger and lighter than those built to the medieval design. Finally, in 1837, the steel plow was invented by the Illinois blacksmith John Deere. It had an all-in-one share and moldboard, just like modern tractor-drawn plows.

How things work

Early Irrigation Machines

For crops to grow they need water. In many parts of the world rainfall is in short supply or falls infrequently. To compensate for this, farmers take water to their crops, a process known as irrigation.

The simplest way to irrigate crops is to transport water in a can or bucket. This is heavy and time-consuming work. Early farmers dug channels to their fields (left) that spread out among the plants to allow water to run between them. However, getting water into the channels was not always easy, particularly if the field was high above the level of the water supply.

Over the centuries several simple but ingenious solutions to this problem were invented. One was the *shaduf*, a seesaw-like contraption with a bucket at one end and a counterweight at the other. Another was the *saqiya*, or Persian water wheel. This was a chain of pots attached to two grooved wheels, one with its lower half in the water source and the other above. When the pots reached the top wheel they emptied into a wooden channel from which the water flowed down to the fields.

Perhaps the most famous device for moving water uphill was the Archimedes screw. Archimedes was a Greek mathematician who lived in the 3rd century B.C.E. His invention consisted of a large screw encased in a watertight covering and open at both ends. The bottom end dipped in the water source and the top opened out at the level of the field. As the screw turned water trapped by pockets of air rose up and flowed from the open upper end. Archimedes' invention is still used in many parts of the world.

Until relatively recently in the history of agriculture, damage caused by insects was something that most farmers just had to put up with. People in ancient China, however, planted chrysanthemums alongside arable crops to deter insects. This companion planting was successful because of a chemical chrysanthemums contain. Today these flowers are grown specifically for that chemical, pyrethrum, which is used to make insecticides.

A scarecrow's human shape unnerves birds. However, birds get used to static scarecrows. For best effect farmers move them around from time to time.

PASTORALIST NOMADS

In dry parts of the world, such as deserts and semideserts, some people travel with herds of animals in search of scarce water and fresh pasture. People that travel with their animals rather than settle in one place are called pastoralist (herding) nomads. Some nomads are on the move constantly, rarely settling for more than a few nights in one place. Others move with the seasons and are only seminomadic.

In east Africa the Maasai people were once largely seminomadic pastoralists. Their dry grassland homes span south-central Kenya and north-central Tanzania. Lush pastures spring up only during the brief rainy season. As a result, some young Maasai men still spend many months away from their main home during the dry season, looking after their family's herd at a distant watering hole. Farther north from the Maasai, where the grasslands become even drier semideserts or desert, many Turkana, Oromo, and Somali people move even more frequently in search of water and fresh pasture.

Asia's most widespread pastoralist nomads were the Mongols. Some groups still

A young Maasai man tends cattle in Kenya. He might stay with the herd for several months at a time, away from the family home.

travel with herds of horses and sheep. Fermented horse's milk, or *koumiss*, is a favorite among nomadic Mongol people. Sheep's milk is drunk fresh or used to make yogurt and cheese. Mutton and sheep's fat are eaten most commonly in winter, when few of the animals are producing milk. Most nomads prefer to avoid killing herd animals, though, since they are valuable providers of milk

A Maasai collects blood from the neck of a cow. This is a way to take food from the animal without killing it.

A 1960s Mongolian herder prepares to milk a horse. Mare's milk is made into a nutritious drink in Mongolia.

and other dairy products, young animals, and also represent a person's wealth.

Nomadic people need portable homes that can be easily packed up and carried on an animal's back. Mongol nomads live in large, round tents called *gers* or *yurts*. In northern Scandinavia the Sami people herd partly domesticated reindeer. The Sami travel with cone-shaped tents called *laitok*.

Today, many nomadic people around the world have been forced or encouraged to settle by governments who want to better control and tax their people. National borders established since the 1900s have deprived many nomads of land they once ranged over.

Although pastoralist nomads are fewer than they once were, a more recent form of nomadic pastoralism is now practiced in the Americas and Australasia. Ranchers and *gauchos* are hired to travel with herds of cattle. Since they are paid a wage, they do not live solely off their animals as other nomads do.

THE AGRICULTURAL REVOLUTION

This 1822 engraving shows farmers discussing the new Leicester sheep produced by Robert Bakewell using selective breeding. These sheep were much fatter than other domestic breeds at the time.

For thousands of years, farming was labor intensive. Landowners employed regular workers, or farmhands, to carry out everyday chores such as milking. At harvest or haymaking times, dozens more people would be hired to help work the land. Early in the 18th century, however, farming began to change radically. People were replaced with machines as the mechanization of the Agricultural Revolution got under way.

The first job to be mechanized was sowing seeds. In 1701, English farmer Jethro Tull (1674–1741) built a machine that dropped seeds into furrows (plowed trench). His invention was followed by other developments that made farming easier. In 1786, Scotsman Andrew Meikle invented a horse-powered threshing machine. Horses walking on a treadmill drove a pulley that rotated a drum. Wheat fed into the gap between the drum and a stationary bar. The wheat had the grain knocked off, or threshed. Previously this job was very laborious. People threshed wheat by beating it with long swinging sticks called flails.

Many more agricultural machines appeared during the 19th century. In 1834, Virginia's Cyrus McCormick (1809–84) patented the first mechanical reaper for harvesting wheat. Before that time standing

24

wheat was cut with scythes, tied by hand into bundles, and carted away. McCormick's horse-drawn device cut the wheat quickly and cleanly. Later models also bound the crop into ready-made sheaves.

The mechanical reaper sped harvesting up many times over. By the 1860s machines very like McCormick's were also being used to cut hay for feeding livestock in the winter.

People and society

Jethro Tull's Seed Drill

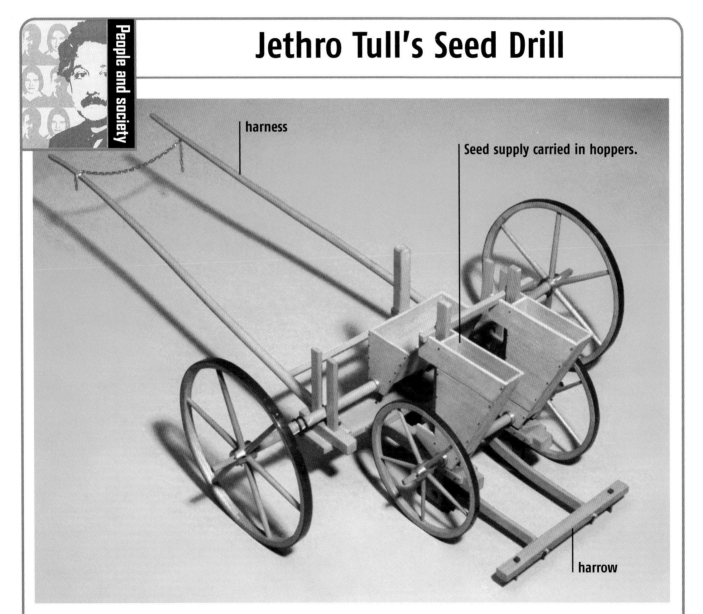

harness

Seed supply carried in hoppers.

harrow

As far back as history records seed was sown by hand, scattered from a bag worn around the neck. The end for this haphazard and wasteful process came in 1701 when the English farmer Jethro Tull developed the first successful mechanized seed drill. Tull's seed drill (model, above) let him sow seeds in straight lines. This made it easier to remove weeds from between the rows. Tull's drill fed seeds into tubes at an even rate. The seeds dropped from the tubes into a furrow made by a colter, or blade. Jethro Tull's seed drill was quickly adopted by other farmers. The principles behind it can still be seen in some seed drills used today. Modern drills also tow a harrow, which draws soil over the seed. Many also dispense fertilizer pellets along with the seeds.

CHANGING PRACTICES

The Agricultural Revolution was not only about using machines. During the 18th and 19th centuries people moved away from the countryside to work in factories. The farmers that remained began to use their land to produce as much food as possible to sell in the growing cities. New machinery was important for this but so were many new farming practices.

The most significant change in farming in the 18th century was the introduction of crop rotation. Land that had previously been plowed and left fallow (rested) for a year to get rid of weeds was now planted with a root crop, such as turnips. Root crops can be easily weeded while growing. Every fourth year, fields farmed by crop rotation were planted with clover. Clover not only provided winter fodder for livestock but also returned nitrogen to the soil.

This painting shows a test of Cyrus McCormick's horse-drawn mechanical reaping machine in 1831.

At the same time as crop rotation was becoming widespread, new breeds of farm animals were starting to appear. The English tenant farmer Robert Bakewell pioneered selective breeding to produce livestock with more desirable characteristics. His efforts led to the creation of longhorn cattle and Leicester sheep. Both animals produced fatty meat, which was popular at the time. Although bred for meat, Leicester sheep were also extremely good wool producers.

Workers dig a U.S. phosphate mine in 1890. Artificial fertilizers largely replaced natural phosphates in the early 20th century.

How things work

The Nitrogen Cycle

All plants and animals need the element nitrogen to make proteins. Proteins are the building blocks of life and are essential for growth.

Nitrogen is the most common gas in the atmosphere, but plants are unable to absorb it directly from air. They need it to be fixed, or converted into more accessible substances by adding other elements to it. Much of the nitrogen taken up by plants is fixed by bacteria in the soil. Some plants, such as peas, beans, and clover, have nitrogen-fixing bacteria living in their roots.

1. Nitrogen gas makes up almost 80 percent of Earth's atmosphere.

2. Nitrogen is fixed by lightning bolts. The energy in the lightning combines nitrogen and oxygen gas in the air to make nitric oxide. This dissolves in rain and falls to the ground as nitric acid.

3. Nitrogen-containing substances become part of the soil as the remains of plants and animals (and their droppings) decay.

4. Bacteria in the soil take nitrogen from the air and the soil. They combine with oxygen and other elements to make compounds called nitrites.

5. Other bacteria add more oxygen to the nitrites to make nitrates, which are more useful to plants.

6. Nitrates in the soil are taken up by plants through their roots. The nitrogen is used to make protein. These proteins are used by animals that eat the plants, and passed on again to meat-eating animals.

7. Other bacteria break down nitrates returning nitrogen gas to the air.

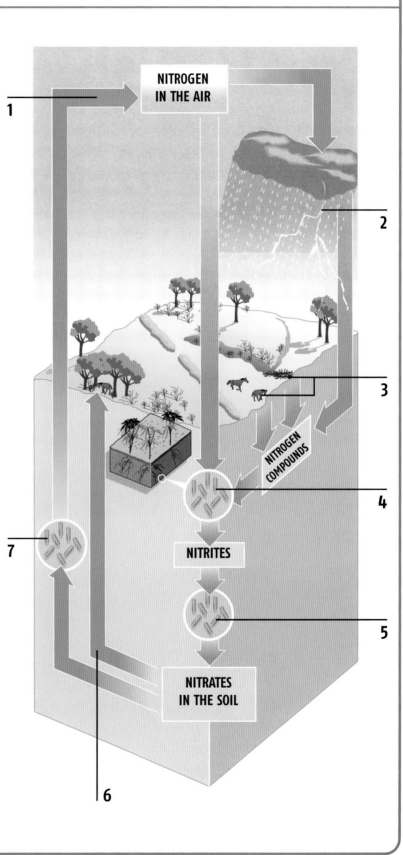

NITROGEN IN THE AIR

1

2

3

NITROGEN COMPOUNDS

4

7

NITRITES

5

6

NITRATES IN THE SOIL

Bakewell's technique of keeping male and female farm animals separate and allowing only certain individuals to mate was continued by his apprentices Charles and Robert Colling. The Colling brothers used these methods to breed shorthorn cattle, which had lean meat. The refinement of the new shorthorn breed coincided with a change in taste among the public for beef without fat. Farmers started to keep shorthorns in preference to longhorn cattle. Shorthorns are still popular with many farmers and ranchers today.

ARTIFICIAL FERTILIZERS

Toward the middle of the 19th century new developments in science began to affect farming. For the first time, scientists were able to make phosphates. These chemicals are important for the growth of plants, but natural phosphates are expensive. Artificial phosphates soon went on sale as artificial fertilizer. Within a few decades, they were joined by ammonia and other nitrogen-based products, which are also used by plants. Artificial fertilizers really came into their own in the early 20th century. By 1910 use of fertilizers had increased global crop yields by an estimated 10 percent.

The Agricultural Revolution had a huge impact in Britain. People were moving into towns and cities to work in factories. They were no longer growing their own produce and needed to buy their groceries.

Key inventions

Fat of the Land

Crops take nutrients from the soil. With each harvest, the crop is removed, and the nutrients are not returned to the soil as they do in the wild as dead plants decay. The soil becomes less fertile, and eventually it can no longer produce healthy crops.

One solution is crop rotation. This process was pioneered in the 18th century by two English landowners called Viscount Townshend and Thomas Coke. After a year of growing barley or wheat on a field, Townshend and Coke turned it over to root crops, such as turnips, or clover. These crops replaced the lost nutrients, and restored the soil for cereals to grow there again. Crop rotation is very effective but in many cases is just not economical. The alternative is to use fertilizers. Fertilizers have been used for a long time. Ancient Greek farmers used dung, while many Native American people used fish to help their crops grow.

Dung is still used as fertilizer, but artificial chemicals are also used. Chemical fertilizers (above) contain substances that are rich in phosphorus and nitrogen and have been available since the 19th century. Artificial phosphates were first made in Britain in 1842. The first nitrogen fertilizers were made in Germany in 1898.

In 1908, German scientist Fritz Haber developed a process for creating ammonia from hydrogen and nitrogen. The Haber process was used to make synthetic fertilizers on a large scale (above). The process is still used today.

Plantations and Slavery

People and society

Long before North America had cowboys and ranches, it had plantations. Plantations were tracts of land given over to the production of one major cash crop. In the United States that crop was typically cotton or sugar cane. The first plantations on what would one day be United States soil appeared in Virginia in the early 1600s. The Virginia plantations produced mostly rice, tobacco, and cotton (above). As new land was taken over, the system spread south into the Mississippi River Valley. There, enormous cotton and sugar estates were developed. By the early 19th century a so-called Cotton Kingdom had grown up around the city of Natchez, Mississippi, while the sugar estates of southeastern Louisiana supported their own wealthy planter society.

Most plantations were owned and managed by a single family but maintained by large numbers of enslaved Africans and their descendants. Plantation owners made vast fortunes from the export of the crops their land produced. The slaves who tended and harvested those crops were given only the most basic food and shelter. Many were whipped or beaten to make them work harder. It is hard to imagine today but slaves were often looked upon as less than human by their owners.

In the Americas, the plantation was the preferred farming method. Plantation owners concentrated on producing a single, valuable crop. In the Caribbean and United States sugar cane was grown widely. Elsewhere, coffee, tea, and cocoa were popular.

Plantations still exist. Now they are tended and harvested by paid workers, not slaves. Some plantations contain plants grown for produce other than food. Rubber trees are harvested for their sap, which contains the latex used in rubber production.

Blown Away

In the great drive west across America huge areas of wilderness were opened up to agriculture. Land that had previously been covered by forest and prairie was suddenly available for the raising of livestock and crops.

The first settlers farmed on a small scale and were relatively scattered. After five to ten years, most found that the land they had plowed and planted with crops was "played out," or exhausted. In fact, it had been drained of nitrogen and other vital nutrients. Unable to sustain themselves on the ever-decreasing yields, they packed up and headed farther west in search of new and untilled soils.

As time passed, the whole American West was turned over to farming and there was nowhere to move on to. Land that had been deserted to the east was resettled and new farms established. Crop failure and soil erosion came to be seen as part of the natural cycle. Then, in the 1930s, the dust bowls set in. Huge areas of Texas, Oklahoma, Nebraska, Iowa, and Kansas were ravaged year after year by twisters and wind storms, which ripped away the loose topsoil and scattered it as dust (left). Crops were destroyed and individual farmers ruined. The land was so badly damaged that agriculture became virtually impossible.

Although the dust bowls were a terrible disaster at the time, they taught farmers a lot about their relationship with the land. Techniques as simple as planting windbreaks and ensuring good ground cover have shown that this type of wind erosion can be avoided completely. Using artificial fertilizer to resupply soil with nutrients can also help. This knowledge has not only helped U.S. farmers but also those around the world. Many areas that suffer from similar wind conditions have prevented dust bowls by learning from the American experience.

FISHING

People have eaten seafood since prehistoric times. The remains of shellfish littered caves along the Mediterranean coast of France that were inhabited by our pre-human ancestors 300,000 years ago. Evidence for our own species eating shellfish dates back almost to its beginning. Caves in South Africa inhabited by people 130,000 years ago contain piles of mollusk shells. By 70,000 years ago people living in that area were also eating fish.

Early methods of fishing were relatively simple. Snails and whelks were gathered from rocks on the shore. Fish were trapped in pools after the tide had fallen.

Early humans also used spears to catch fish, both along the coast and from lakes and rivers inland. Bone fish hooks suggest that people had started angling by 40,000 years ago.

Fishing with hooks, spears, or traps is a bit hit or miss and yields only limited amounts of food. Nets can catch many fish at one time. The oldest fishing nets yet found are about 12,000 years old and were discovered in modern-day Israel. Thrown by hand over shoals of fish in the shallows, these nets were made of knotted rope. The rope was made with vines and weighted at the edges with stones. By 10,000

Fishing from the shore was one of the earliest forms of fishing with a net. This simple but effective method is still practiced. These people are fishing in East Timor, Southeast Asia.

years ago people in Africa, South America, and Southeast Asia were attaching floats made from gourds to their nets to keep them afloat.

HARVESTING THE SEAS

For millennia, fishing was limited to inland waters or the coast. It was not until the development of more seaworthy boats that fishing in open water became possible. The ancient Greeks and Romans discovered fishing grounds in the Mediterranean. Later, the Vikings developed sea fishing in the North Atlantic. They made their nets of nettle and hemp twine. Lines of nettle-hemp were tied to a thicker main line with clove-hitch knots. The hanging lines were meshed

Salmon Ladder

How things work

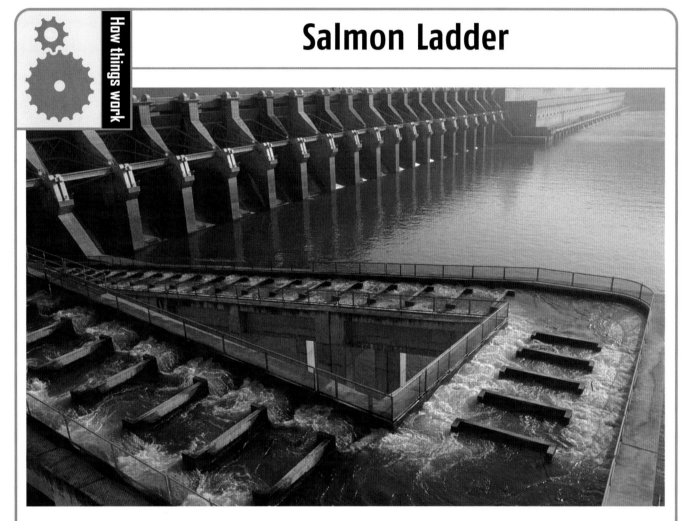

Salmon are famous for their migrations up rivers to breed. Every year these fish travel from their ocean feeding grounds back to the rivers and lakes where they were born. They battle determinedly up rapids and leap over waterfalls. Today, however, people have blocked many salmon rivers with impassable dams. Unable to reach their spawning grounds, the salmon cannot breed. The salmon ladder (above) was invented to help migrating salmon get past these artificial obstacles. The flow of water from the bottom of the ladder attracts the fish toward it. The fish come to a series of small, artificial waterfalls, interspersed with resting pools. The waterfalls are low enough for the salmon to jump over. They make their way up to the top of the dam and into the river beyond.

Whaling

Commercial whaling is now banned by international treaty but was once a huge industry. Thousands of men were employed on fleets of specially designed ships. Whales were hunted for their meat, oil, and blubber. The ivory-like baleen plates of the large filter-feeding animals were used to make whalebone corsets, among other things.

Before the 19th century whaling was a very dangerous business. Whalers had to row beside the massive animals, killing them with harpoons thrown by hand. In the 1860s, the first steam-powered whaling ship was launched in Norway. This vessel had a harpoon gun mounted at the front. Attached to the ship by a long steel cable, the harpoon contained a grenade, which exploded when it entered the whale. As the decades passed whaling ships got even bigger. In 1925, the ships were floating factories, processing the whales on board. Soon many whale species were on the edge of extinction. The International Whaling Commission was established in 1946 to conserve whale stocks. After years of protests by environmental campaigners commercial hunting of larger whales (above) was banned in 1986. However, Japan, Iceland, and Norway are still allowed to hunt certain species for scientific purposes.

together using a knot called the sheet bend. Although the material is different, people in many parts of the world still make nets in this way. The Vikings also hunted a new quarry, whales. These air-breathing mammals were driven ashore by men in boats and butchered where they were stranded. In the 17th century the Japanese began to use gigantic hemp nets for whaling. Large groups of people in boats drove the whales into nets out at sea. Once entangled, the whales were killed with harpoons.

By that time trawler fishing was well established in Europe. The first boats to drag large trawler nets behind them appeared in Portugal in the 13th century. Before long, similar nets were being used on large sailing ships out at sea. In 1497 John Cabot landed at Newfoundland. Many historians believe he was guided there by reports from English fishers. They had fished the huge shoals of cod in the region.

TYPES OF NET

The structure of fishing net mesh has hardly changed since the 16th century. What is different is the

structures of the nets. Early trawlers towed simple baglike nets held open by a single beam. Trawler nets are now much more complicated. They have a variety of devices to make them more efficient at catching fish.

Trawler fishing is one of the most common methods of catching fish at sea but it is far from the only one. Before World War I (1914–18), fishers around the world had started using a new type of net called a purse seine. The purse seine is used to trap whole shoals of fish. The edge of the net is held at the surface by floats, while the bulk of it hangs below. Once a shoal of fish has been located, the boat circles it, letting out the net as it goes. When the circle is complete, the gaps at the bottom and side are pulled shut like a drawstring purse. The net is slowly winched back onto the boat, along with the shoal of fish inside it.

Fishing nets work either by trapping or entangling fish. Trawl nets and purse seine nets are essentially gigantic bags that trap fish inside them. They work because their mesh is too small for most fish to swim through.

Gill nets have a large mesh and work by entangling fish. Like purse seine nets, their top edge is held at the water's surface by floats. The rest hangs below like an invisible curtain.

Gill nets are used by Canadian fishers for catching salmon in lakes or near river mouths. They

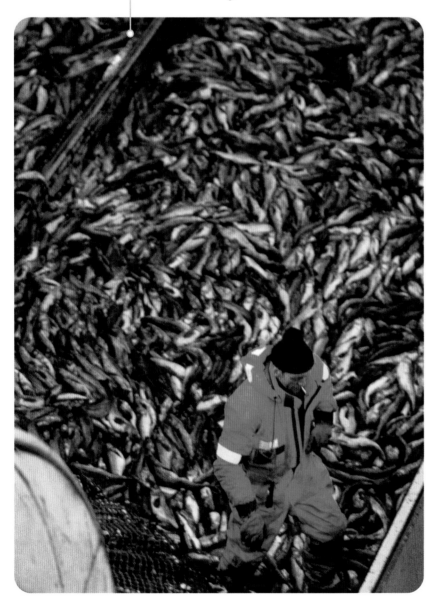

A fisher stands on deck among a catch of thousands of pollack in Alaska. Many modern fishing vessels such as this are factory ships. The catch is processed on board and landed ready for sale.

How things work

Trawler Fishing

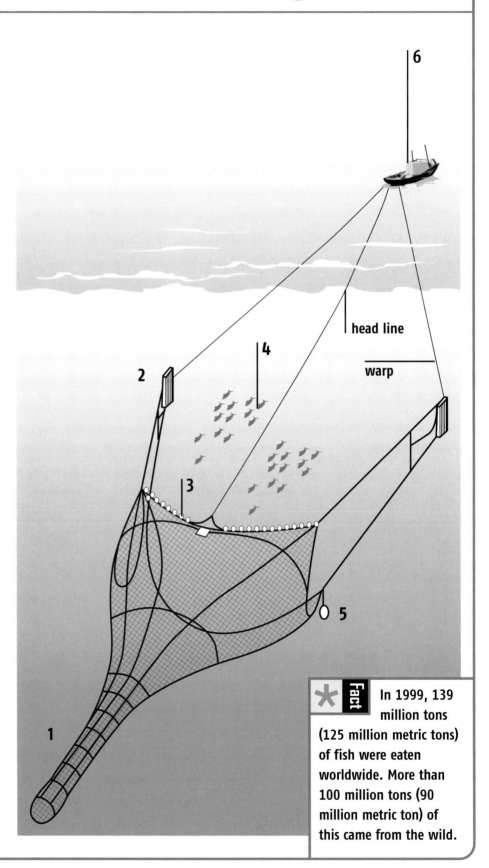

head line

warp

2

4

3

1

5

6

Taking fish from the sea requires special equipment. Trawler fishers tow their nets from behind their boats (6). In the mid-19th century most trawlers used nets with a beam along the top. The beam held the net open but limited the size of the net that could be used. In the 1870s, otter boards (2) were invented. These moved apart from one another as they were towed, allowing the mouth of a net to be opened much wider. Most trawler fishers still use nets with otter boards today. Floats (3) are attached to the top of the net's mouth and weights (5) to the bottom to hold it open vertically. Sometimes an extra otter board is attached to the head line to give further lift to the top of the mouth. The net itself is shaped like a funnel with a closed end. As the boat moves, fish (4) pass through the wide mouth and are forced ever tighter together. Eventually they are trapped at the cod end (1). When the net is pulled in, the cod end is dragged on to the boat. It is opened, spilling the fish on to the deck for sorting by the fishers.

★ Fact In 1999, 139 million tons (125 million metric tons) of fish were eaten worldwide. More than 100 million tons (90 million metric ton) of this came from the wild.

Recreational fishing is a popular sport in North America and Europe. These people are fishing a dam on the Laurel River, Kentucky.

allowed to drift behind a boat to catch surface fish such as tuna or are sunk to the bottom with weights to catch fish such as cod. The latter method is relatively harmless to other sea life but lines at the surface kill thousands of sea birds, including albatrosses.

FINDING FISH

Fishers have many techniques to help them find fish. Before the 20th century they used natural clues such as diving sea birds to lead them to shoals. Fishers now have a variety of fish-finding equipment at their disposal. Sonar was developed in World War II (1939–45) to locate submarines. It is now used widely to search out shoals of fish. Aerial surveillance and even satellite images are employed by some of the larger ships and fleets.

can be operated by a single person on a small boat. Gill nets are let out from one end, left to float for a few hours, then slowly drawn in and the fish extracted.

Use of gill nets in the open ocean is often called drift netting. The nets are left to drift freely, hence the name. Sometimes the nets are fixed by weights to the seabed. Many people oppose using drift nets because they catch all type of sea life. In addition to the intended fish, dolphins, turtles, and even whales become entangled in the gigantic curtains of netting. Because the nets are left for so long, these creatures drown long before they can be detected and freed.

Another type of fishing that often hits the news is long-lining. This method uses baited hooks attached by short cords to a single line. Long-lining has been in use since the time of the Vikings. The lines are either

All of this new technology combined with bigger, stronger nets has left fish with few places to hide. Fish stocks in many parts of the oceans are dwindling. Catches are getting smaller. One area that has profited from this problem is aquaculture. Farmed fish and other seafood is becoming ever more widely available. Raising fish in this way may give wild stocks a chance to recover from overfishing. Aquaculture also causes problems. Waste from fish farms may pollute the surrounding area. Breeding areas for fish may be developed for aquaculture, and wild fish are still caught to feed farmed fish.

FISH FARMS

The old saying that "there are plenty more fish in the sea" is no longer accurate. The demand for fish is growing rapidly and improvements in fishing vessels and nets means that many ocean fisheries are depleted severely. Some formerly abundant stocks have disappeared entirely. Fish farming and other forms of aquaculture offer an alternative to taking fish and other seafood from the wild.

Fish farming dates back more than 4,000 years. The oldest known records for it come from ancient China. Artificial pools were dug alongside rivers. Carp and gray mullet entered the pools and spawned. The fish farmers fed the young fish with silk worms and animal droppings until they were big enough to eat. The Romans also dug ponds for storing fish, as did medieval monks in Europe.

Before the widespread improvement of roads in Europe in the 19th century, fresh fish was a scarce and valuable commodity inland.

Ancient and medieval fish farming concentrated on freshwater fish. Today a wide variety of saltwater species are raised as well. Red snappers are farmed commercially off Puerto Rico. New Zealand snappers and mulloway are raised along the

Workers harvesting farmed catfish in Mississippi. Catfish are raised in pools and caught in nets for killing and processing. Catfish farming is a big business in the southern United States.

coast of Australia. In the Mediterranean and around Hawaii there are even saltwater farms for tuna.

Perhaps the most farmed fish today is the Atlantic salmon. Even as little as 50 years ago salmon was an expensive delicacy. Now it is farmed in such large quantities that it has become an inexpensive fish. Salmon are kept in submerged cages (main picture, in Scotland). The salmon farming industry is worth more than half a billion dollars a year worldwide.

Aquaculture extends beyond just farming fish. Among the other types of animal raised commercially are crustaceans such as shrimp and crayfish. Shrimp farming is big business in many parts of the world. Thailand produces around a quarter of a million tons of black tiger prawns every year, bringing huge revenues into the country. The prawns are raised in flooded fields along the coast that were once used for growing rice.

Many other shellfish are farmed commercially. Oysters are raised in mesh bags along the shores of Canada and Scotland. Mussels are cultivated suspended along ropes, so they can be pulled easily from the water for harvesting. Even sponges and seaweeds are farmed.

GETTING INTENSIVE

Modern combine harvesters gather and sort crops at a rate and on a scale that was unimaginable when food was harvested using simple tools.

The mechanization of farming began during the Agricultural Revolution. The power for these early devices was provided by horses. In the 1860s, the first steam-powered machines appeared on farms. Massive and bulky steam engines were too heavy to drive over fields. They flattened the soil and got bogged down in mud.

However, engineers still found ways to put steam to use on farms. So-called balancing plows were strung between two engines on opposite sides of a field. The engines powered pulleys that dragged the plow toward them. When it reached one engine, the balancing plow was tipped. Blades facing the opposite way then engaged, and the second engine began pulling the plow back across the field to the other side.

Steam engines powered other agricultural machines, such as threshers. Farmers who bought the new engines needed fewer horses and horse pastures could now be used for growing more crops.

Not everybody was convinced by steam engines. People in smaller farms found the expense of large machinery outweighed the benefits. They kept their horses.

TRACTORS TAKE OVER
In 1917, car manufacturer Henry Ford (1863–1947) began producing the gasoline-driven Model F Fordson tractor. Fitted with steel

Greening the Desert

California's Imperial Valley (above, seen from space) is a miracle of modern agriculture. A century ago the Imperial Valley was a very dry desert. Today it is lush with vines and orange groves. The transformation is due entirely to people. The All-American Canal brings water from the Colorado River 80 miles (128 km) west to irrigate the desert. Imperial Valley is an American example of a global phenomenon of mass irrigation. In Egypt large sections of the desert have been turned over to farming, using water pumped from wells to supply sprinkler systems. Australian farmers build dams across rivers on their rain-starved land to provide reservoirs for watering crops.

It is not only individuals or governments getting involved. The United Nations (UN) has launched a program in Africa to prevent fertile land from drying out. Using local knowledge to identify water sources and drought-resistant crops, the UN is helping people reclaim land lost through unsuitable farming practices and soil erosion. Farmers from South Africa to Mali are starting to see barren land grow green again.

 Fact The area of irrigated land around the world is more than twice that of Texas. In the United States alone, an area of farmland the size of Kansas is irrigated.

Key inventions

Harvesting Made Easy

The self-propelled combine harvester was invented in the late 1800s. Today these massive machines are a common sight in many parts of the developed world. Their existence has changed the landscape. Combines harvest huge areas of crops, and small fields are often combined into one. Modern combine harvesters (1) not only pick cereals but also separate them into grains and straw.

As the vehicle moves forward it causes the hexagonal, twined reel on the front to rotate. This folds the crop toward the cutter, which slices the plant at the root. Behind the cutter is a rotating shaft called the auger. This is a drumlike spiral that guides the cut crop backward and toward the center of the harvesting machine. From there it is lifted upward on a short conveyor belt to the inside of the harvester. Once inside, the cut crop is ground between a large rotating drum and a curved piece of metal. This knocks the grain and chaff (unwanted husks) from the stalks. The mixture of grain, chaff, and stalks is then passed over a device called a straw walker. The grain and chaff fall through slots in the walker, which shakes as it moves. The chaff is blown free of the grain by a fan beneath the walker. The straw stalks pass to the back of the combine, from where they are thrown out. The grain collects in the bottom of the harvester. An elevator belt transports it to the grain tank. Once the tank is full the grain empties into a trailer via a long tube (2), called the unloading auger, on the side of the combine. Large trucks (3) carry the harvest away.

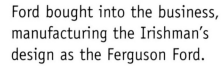

wheels, it was lightweight but capable of heavy work. There had been gasoline tractors before but none that combined the lightness and power of the Model F. It went into mass production. Soon farms all over North America and Europe owned one of the new tractors.

Ford became the world's biggest tractor manufacturer, but soon they had competition from Harry Ferguson, the son of a farmer from Northern Ireland. Ferguson developed a hydraulic system for mounting farm implements on tractors. His invention was a great success. Previous tractors pulled plows and other machinery in the same way animals did. Ferguson's system allowed farmers to attach tools to the back of the tractor to make a single unit. This put more pressure on the rear wheels, improving grip. Farm machinery attachments could be carried rather than dragged from the field. Ferguson sold his tractors cheaply but made extra money on his range of mechanized tools.

Ford bought into the business, manufacturing the Irishman's design as the Ferguson Ford.

Massey Harris also made tractors, under the name Ferguson Harris. Massey Harris later became Massey Ferguson, today one of the biggest manufacturers of farm equipment in the United States.

A NEW NEED FOR WATER

Irrigation was once an issue only for farmers in dry countries. However, modern farming practices need a lot of water, and much of the world's farms now need an extra supply of water for crops.

Modern irrigation is achieved in one of three ways. The most common is surface irrigation, where water is trickled into channels dug between the crop rows. Excess water runs off into drains. In places where water is plentiful, such as the eastern United States, sprinklers are used to spray crops. Some sprinklers move on wheels from one side of the field to another. Others rotate, spraying water around them in a circle. The third and least common type of irrigation is subsurface irrigation. This involves inserting a layer of watertight material just beneath the crops' roots to hold water and keep them moist.

There are problems associated with irrigation. River water and water from underground is much saltier than rainwater. Salts crystallize on the soil when water evaporates. This slowly but surely makes the land less fertile. Much

Mass production of gasoline tractors in the 20th century brought increased mechanization to farms throughout much of the United States and Europe.

farmland in places such as Kansas and Texas has been lost in this way in the past. A build-up of salt in the soil can be avoided by providing enough drainage.

LIVESTOCK FARMING

Before World War II (1939–45) livestock was raised and cared in much the same way as it had been for centuries. In the 1940s, animal husbandry industry went through a profound change as the ideas behind intensive production were applied to livestock.

The first animals to be farmed intensively were chickens. Coops with runs became old fashioned, and chickens were housed in gigantic sheds. The chickens were held in lines of cages called batteries. Battery chickens are fed on powdered food. Their eggs fall from the chickens directly on to the sloping floor of the cages. Then the eggs roll out into channels for collection.

Pigs, turkeys, and dairy cattle were the next animals to be farmed intensively. Like chickens,

Key inventions

Milking Machines

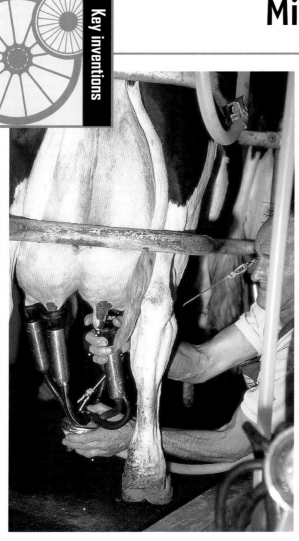

Devices for milking cows have existed since the 19th century. The first milking machine was patented in 1860 by an American engineer L. O. Colvin. It consisted of four rubber teat cups attached to a vacuum chamber on the side of a pail. The vacuum chamber was hand operated in the same way as bellows. Suction drew the milk from the cow's teats and into the bucket. In 1889, Colvin's design was incorporated into an elaborate system by a Scottish farmer named William Murchland. He employed a column of water to create the vacuum and used a complex network of iron pipes. Murchland created a system by which an entire shed could be connected up to milk several cows at a time. Although efficient, Murchland's milking machine suffered from a serious flaw. The continuous vacuum caused the cows pain. Sometimes the animals suffered internal bleeding and the milk became contaminated with blood. In 1895 another Scot, Alexander Shields, overcame this problem by designing a milking machine system with a pulsating device. Shields' device caused regular punctuations in the vacuum, temporarily relieving the pressure on the cows' teats. Although improved, today's milking machines (left) are built along similar lines to Shields' design, incorporating the principles of suction and pulsation.

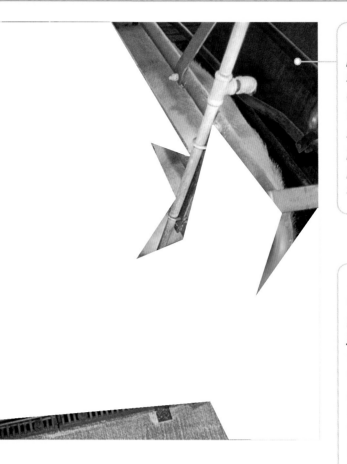

Many farmers keep pregnant or suckling sows in a farrowing crate. This keeps the mother from squashing the piglets but many people think the system is cruel.

After the discovery of DDT in 1939 people had for the first time a cheap and easy way to control insect pests. Just 34 years later, the use of DDT was banned in the United States. People had realized the chemical was poisoning wildlife.

they were moved into indoor pens and fed on meal (ground-up food) or pellets produced in factories.

Intensification allowed farmers greater control over their animals. Farmers increased production by regulating animals' diets and surroundings. Different types of farm animal were now separated and, in the case of pigs, individuals kept apart. Separation reduced the risk of contagious disease.

Since the late 1960s many intensive farmers have fed antibiotics to their animals routinely to reduce disease risk. Growth hormones are commonly used in the United States to increase meat production. These hormones make animals grow much faster so they can be slaughtered at an earlier age.

GREATER USE OF CHEMICALS

While livestock farming was undergoing the intensive revolution, arable farming was also receiving a boost. The insecticide DDT was invented in 1939. Six years later scientists developed the first selective weedkiller, called 2,4-D. These discoveries and those that followed them ushered in a new era. Crop spraying wiped out insect pests or stopped competition from other plants. Yields increased. Arable farmers became as dependent on chemicals as they were on machines.

Farmers were producing more food than ever before from the land. Unfortunately, the miracle soon tarnished. DDT builds up in the bodies of creatures, especially

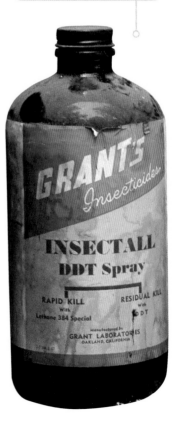

Crop Spraying

Making a profit from arable farming involves much more than just planting crops in the ground. Competition from other plants must be minimized and pests deterred or destroyed. For thousands of years arable farmers weeded their fields by hand. Wild plants that competed with crops for light and nutrients were picked out one by one. Weeding fields by hand was time consuming and back breaking. People frightened away some creatures that might feed on the crops. Many other pests, such as insects, were simply accepted. There was little that people could do to get rid of them.

Today's arable farmers use a wide range of chemicals. Herbicides and pesticides have relegated weeding and crop pests to the past. Most of these chemicals are available in liquid form and are distributed by spraying. Farmers have the choice of spraying their fields by hand, from tanks mounted on the back of tractors, or even from the air. In places where large areas of land are covered by crops, helicopters and light airplanes are used for the job. Pilots who make a living operating aircraft for spraying call themselves crop dusters.

those that are high up the food chain like eagles and coyotes. Although most animals were unaffected, birds of prey were decimated. The chemical makes their eggs very weak, and many eggs broke in the nest before they could hatch. The U.S. government banned DDT in 1973. Herbicides, (plant-killing chemicals) also damage nature by reducing the range of wild plants.

ORGANIC FARMING

Chicken feed on an organic farm. People will pay more to eat these birds. Many think organic food tastes better than other foods.

In recent years many shoppers have turned away from food farmed intensively in favor of organic produce. Unlike crops on most farms, food produced organically is treated with a minimum of artificial chemicals. Use of synthetic fertilizers, herbicides, and pesticides is controlled. Organic livestock is raised without growth hormones and fed on natural foodstuffs. Genetically modified organisms are banned.

In order to market their produce as organic, farmers have either to prove that they have always farmed organically or go through a conversion period during which their land is farmed to tight organic guidelines. Organic farming tends to produce less food per acre, but organic produce often attracts a higher price than that produced intensively.

The fear some shoppers have of the health risks connected to intensively farmed foods is sometimes exaggerated. But there are examples where modern farming practices have caused danger to consumers. BSE, or mad cow disease, is a brain disease that was unheard of before the 1980s. It is caused by feeding cattle with pellets containing contaminated meat

Of far more significance than the health benefits of organic food, is the effect organic farming has on the environment. By tackling pests and weeds with chemicals, intensive farms are often empty of virtually all wildlife. Most pesticides and herbicides kill far more than just their intended victims. Farms with no wildflowers or insects rarely have many birds and mammals. Organic farms encourage wildlife by allowing insects and wild plants to thrive. Organic farmers may experience lower crop yields, but their surroundings are richer in flora and fauna.

Organic farming may be more natural than its intensive counterpart but the people who practice it are just as busy as other farmers, if not more so. Without herbicides, weeds that damage crops have to be removed by hand. Many organic farmers harvest their crops manually, instead of using machines.

Pest control on organic farms is achieved mainly by crop-rotation—growing crops in a different area from where they were grown the year before. This effectively starves crop pests to death, particularly those that live in the soil. When crops are returned after a year or more, large populations of pests that previously caused problems may no longer be there. Some organic farmers reduce their pest problems by choosing pest-resistant varieties of their chosen crop.

Organic food is often certified as such by an organization. The United States has many accredited certification bodies. Most other countries have one main body. In order to qualify for certification, farmers have to prove that their land is farmed organically. Often they need to show that the livestock they raise is well treated and slaughtered humanely. Farther down the line, food-processing companies that sell food labeled as organic must prove that not only the main ingredients but also added flavorings are produced organically.

and bone. That came sheep infected with a similar brain disease, called scrapie. Beef products infected with BSE have been blamed for a rise in cases of a strain of Creutzfeldt-Jakob disease, a human brain disorder. BSE would not have occurred if all meat was farmed organically. To many consumers, organic foods (right) seem more natural and wholesome.

Puffed Cereals

ORGANIC GRADE

The Soil Association symbol is your guarantee of food grown organically without artificial chemicals or fertilisers.

flavour by nature

NEW TECHNIQUES

Considering how long people have been farming, it seems amazing that there is still room for advances. People continue to invent new and better ways to grow crops and raise livestock for food. Scientists around the world are working on research programs aimed at making agriculture more productive and profitable.

During the 20th century, huge advances were made in developing plants and animals that grew larger and faster. Through selective breeding, farmers and scientists created ever more vigorous and high-yielding strains of crops and livestock. In 1960, the average dairy cow gave 78 pints (37 liters) of milk a year; today, that has more than tripled to 245 pints (116 liters). The average chicken laid four eggs a week then. Now it produces one every day. Wheat has been so much improved that an acre (0.4 hectares) now yields three times as much grain as it did in 1925.

Selective breeding was not the only thing that increased yields. The increase in the development and use of farm chemicals played a significant role. In the 1960s a dramatic rise in the global population led the United Nations Food and Agriculture Organization to launch the so-called Green Revolution. The aim of this

An ultrafine micropipette is used to take material out of a living cell. Scientists use micromanipulation techniques such as this to genetically engineer cells.

program was to end hunger and famine. While the program only partly achieved its aim, it spurred agrochemical companies to develop more efficient fertilizers and pesticides. Scientists helped by creating higher yield varieties of cereals, such as corn and rice.

ARTIFICIAL INSEMINATION
The advances made in selective breeding of livestock have been aided by the widespread adoption of artificial insemination (AI). AI involves collecting sperm from a male animal and using it to impregnate females. The

How things work

Biological Control

The rising popularity of organic food and consumer fears about traces of insecticide remaining on crops has led farmers to look for new ways of dealing with pests. One of the latest developments is a return to the oldest method of all, biological control. Biological control uses the natural enemies of animal and plant pests to reduce their numbers. Creatures that eat pests are introduced among crops to hunt the pests down. Ladybirds may be spread through crops infested with aphids, or pirate bugs used to control outbreaks of mites.

Weeds can be dealt with in a similar manner. Knapweed can be treated by introducing seed-head weevils. Leaf beetles (above) are approved for control of saltcedar in the United States. As well as predators, creatures that kill from the inside are also used in biological control. Roundworms are particularly effective. These tiny animals work their way into a pest's body and eat it alive. There are almost as many types of roundworms as there are insects. By using the right roundworm, virtually any insect pest can be targeted.

Breeding animals such as this Hereford bull were once taken from farm to farm to make cows pregnant. Modern commercial breeding is done by artificial insemination.

technique was first developed in 1780. New technology has made AI more useful and practical. Semen stored in liquid nitrogen can be kept fresh for years and used for AI long after the donor has died. Later generations of livestock can now be bred directly from long-dead animals with valuable features. AI also makes transportation less of a problem. Semen from a bull in the United States can now be used to impregnate a cow in Australia without any risk of the semen being damaged during the journey.

Other technological advances have transformed the raising of farm animals and plants. Chicken eggs no longer need to be incubated by a brood hen before hatching. Instead, machines called incubators keep eggs at exactly the right temperature almost from the moment they are laid. Other poultry can also be brought to hatching in this way.

Hydroponics is a method of growing plants without using soil. This has proved useful in regions where land is poor or infertile. Not all crops lend themselves to being grown in this way. However, many vegetables have proven very responsive to hydroponics and are now grown commercially by this method, among them cucumbers, lettuces, and tomatoes.

single-celled fungus. Other tiny organisms, bacteria, have been used for centuries to turn milk into yogurt or cheese. People used these organisms but did not even know that they were there. In the 17th century the first microscopes powerful enough to see yeasts and bacteria were invented. People began to understand the processes that they and their ancestors had used for so long.

Microorganisms are used widely in biotechnology today. Many are grown in massive vats called fermenters, which may be as tall as apartment blocks. Modern fermenters are controlled by computer, which ensures that conditions are perfect for the microorganisms to thrive and so generate more products.

Biotechnology is being applied in an increasing number of ways every year. Many plants, such as orchids, are grown by a branch of biotechnology called tissue

Once sperm has been extracted from a prize bull, it is stored in liquid nitrogen to keep it fresh. Frozen sperm is sent around the world to fertilize whole herds of cows.

BIOTECHNOLOGY

Biotechnology is the exploitation of living organisms for processes that are beneficial to people. In simple terms, this usually means taking plants, animals, microorganisms, or fungi and making them produce useful substances. One early application of biotechnology was adding yeast to bread to make it rise. Yeast is a

Annie is a cloned Jersey cow. Her cells were given genes that protect against mastitis, a serious infection of the teats. Cloning is a new field of biotechnology that may have a large effect on farming.

Key inventions

Hydroponics

Growing crops in the open has two main drawbacks. Firstly, the local climate limits the types of plants that can be grown. Secondly, the crops can often be produced for only part of the year, depending on the seasons. Hydroponics overcomes both of these problems. Plants are grown indoors, where temperature and light exposure can be controlled by people. In addition, crops are grown in water rather than soil. *Hydroponics* means "water working" in Greek. It is an accurate name since the water does almost all of the work. Water saturated with minerals the plant needs for growth takes the place of soil in every respect apart from physical support. That is provided by a solid medium, such as crushed rocks.

Hydroponically grown plants can be raised all year round anywhere on Earth. At the moment, Canada and the Netherlands are leading the way in commercial hydroponics, although several other cold-climate countries are developing their own industries. The ability to produce summer crops in winter is the main attraction to growers. Hydroponics has an additional advantage over traditional farming: The growing environment is enclosed, so there is no risk of attack from pests or weeds. Hydroponic farmers do not need to use expensive herbicides or pesticides. By avoiding using them, they cause less direct pollution than conventional arable farms. However, hydroponic farms use more fuel.

culture. In this technique, a few cells are taken from an adult plant and grown on a nutrient-rich gel in a petri dish. When the bundle of cells reaches a certain size it is divided and the halves grown again. In this way many new plants can be grown from a single parent. Tissue culture is used commercially by many companies that sell plants. Unilever produces oil palms using tissue culture. The palms are grown in plantations in Indonesia and other hot countries to provide oil for cooking and the manufacture of soap.

GENETIC ENGINEERING

One of the most recent techniques to be applied to the food industry is genetic engineering. It produces the kinds of results you might expect if it was possible to breed different species with each other. Genetic engineering transfers desirable characteristics from one species into another. This is done by extracting a section of DNA (one or more genes) responsible for the characteristic. This DNA is added to that of another organism, which may be a crop plant or farm animal.

How things work

Transgenic Organs

In the past farm animals were kept for food and milk. Today they are also raised for very different reasons. Pigs are now kept not just for pork but as hosts for growing organs. The organs of a normal pig would be rejected by a human recipient. Pigs that have been genetically engineered to have tissue identical to a human could be used to supply healthy hearts (above, a genetically human pig heart), livers, and kidneys for transplanting. Pigs are used because they are a similar size to people. Transgenic pigs have been bred and a few people with liver failure have already been kept alive with pig organs while they were waiting for a human donor.

The thought of transplanting organs from animals is horrible to many people. However, healthy human organs are hard to find and many sufferers never get a chance for a transplant operation.

Transplanting organs grown in animals has risks. Some scientists fear that it could cause new diseases. Of particular concern is the possibility of animal viruses being passed on to humans.

GENETIC ENGINEERING

Genetic engineering, or genetic modification (GM), is the altering of the genes inside plants or animals. Genes control how an organism looks and, in some cases, how it behaves. By changing or adding genes, scientists can alter organisms to make them more useful. To achieve the same changes by selective breeding would take many generations, and in many cases it may not be possible at all. Genetic engineers have freedoms not enjoyed by previous breeders. For example genes that enable arctic fish to resist the cold have been added to cereal plants to make them tolerant to frosts.

Research into genetic engineering began in the 1970s. Early results were modest. It took time for the benefits of this field of study to be realized. Today, many kinds of plants and animals exist that have been improved by genetic engineering. Herbicide-resistant soybeans, cotton, and corn are now

Protestors disrupt a trial planting of a genetically modified (GM) crop. Many people will not eat GM food, because of health fears or environmental concerns.

available to farmers. Rice has been engineered to produce more vitamins and iron. Sweet potatoes have been altered to make them resistant to devastating viruses. Many plants have been changed to cope with extreme weather conditions. These are just some of the genetically modified organisms now available. In the future, genetic engineers hope to produce bananas that contain human vaccines against infectious diseases, fish that grow faster, fruit trees that yield at an earlier age, and plants that make plastics with completely new properties.

The benefits of genetic engineering are clear. By using this technology people will be able to make crops that are hardier and more productive. Livestock may be less susceptible to disease. All of these things will help farmers get more from the land. They could even help combat starvation by making it easier for poor countries to produce enough food.

Despite the obvious benefits GM food is often controversial. Some GM crops have had genes added that make them immune to the effects of certain pesticides. There are fears that these modified plants could cross-pollinate with wild plants and create so-called "superweeds." The companies that create genetically modified crops patent them, so only they can produce seeds. The companies also often sell the chemical pesticides that have to be used to help their patented plants grow. The

debate continues whether this system actually works. Some people are worried that these companies might become too powerful, especially in developing countries.

Many people worry about the potential impact of GM foods on human health.

Soybeans have been modified to suit many needs. The large bean is used in tofu, while the smaller, round bean is used for fermentation. The egg-shaped bean is unmodified.

Nobody can say for certain that eating altered plants and animals is safe. Only time will tell whether these fears are unfounded.

As well as environmental and health issues, genetic engineering raises ethical problems. Many feel that it is wrong to tamper with nature in this way. The very idea of mixing genes from plants and animals worries many people, not least vegetarians and people who hold strong religious beliefs.

PREPARATION AND PRESERVATION

Once harvested or butchered, fresh food has a tendency to slowly spoil or rot. Before the advent of farming, people ate food almost as they found it. As long as it was good to eat when they found it, there was no problem. When people settled and became farmers, things changed. Crops took time to grow and were seasonal. Livestock could not be relied on to survive through lean times such as drought or winter. If a settled population was going to be safe from hunger, it needed to have a back-up food supply.

USING HEAT

One of the earliest methods used for preserving food was to dry it in the sun. Dried food lasts longer and can be eaten as it is or added to water to make a broth or stew. Drying is such a simple and efficient way of preserving food that we still use it today: Jerky is dried meat. Drying can also be used to concentrate and enhance flavor, as in the case of sun-dried raisins or tomatoes.

Another ancient way to keep food from going bad is to smoke it. Like drying, smoking works by

Nobody knows when people first started cooking food. The simplest way of doing this is to heat the food over an open fire. Cooking makes food safer to eat by killing any disease-causing organisms. It also makes it easier for our bodies to digest the food.

Brewing and Winemaking

HLB

BEAUFORT CONVEYORS

Alcoholic beverages such as beer and wine are drunk around the world every day of the year. Without the help of a fungus, they would never exist. The alcohol in these drinks is produced by yeast. Yeast forms alcohol by breaking down sugars. Yeast also produces carbon dioxide gas, which is why some beers and wines are fizzy.

The process by which yeast makes alcohol is known as fermentation. Brewers add yeast to a mash of malted barley, hops, and water to make beer. This is done in large heated vats called *tuns* (above). Wine is fermented by yeasts that grow naturally on the skin of grapes. It is stored in oak barrels for about a year before being drunk.

The Lure of Spice

Spices are plant products added to food to alter or improve its flavor. The most familiar spice is pepper (being harvested above). There are dozens of others. People have been using spices since prehistory. The first references to them are made in some of the earliest known writings. Stone tablets chiseled in Assyria more than 4,000 years ago tell of the gods drinking sesame-flavored wine before they created Earth.

Many spices came from plants that grew only in particular places. In ancient times these plants were very valuable. Whole communities survived on their trade. Frail ships carried spices across the oceans from exotic islands. Camel caravans plodded hundreds of miles to bring spices to markets for sale. In the Old Testament of the Bible, the Book of Genesis tells of Joseph being sold to a spice caravan by his brothers. Centuries later, the Queen of Sheba took a gift of camels bearing spices when she visited King Solomon.

For 2,000 years the spice trade was controlled by Arab peoples. They transported cloves, pepper, and ginger from the east, where they bought them from merchants. The source of the spices was kept secret from Europeans. To deter others from searching for spices themselves, Arab traders told terrifying stories of monsters and other dangers on the route.

In 1271, Italian adventurer Marco Polo (1254–1324) began a long adventure through Asia. He returned 24 years later with tales of the great ports and spice markets of Java and India. Over the next two centuries European explorers battled to reach these places by ship. The first to succeed were the Portuguese, who claimed Sri Lanka before continuing to the Spice Islands (eastern Indonesia). Seeking a quicker passage, Christopher Columbus (1451–1506) headed west. He never got to the Spice Islands but discovered America instead.

Today spices are commonplace and affordable for most people. Spices may have lost their glamor and mystery, but their place in history is assured. Without spices, the age of exploration might never have happened, and the world we live in would be a very different place.

removing moisture. Microorganisms that spoil food need moisture to survive. Smoking alters flavor and is best suited for fish or meat. Oily fish such as herring and mackerel are commonly smoked. Ham and bacon are the most common smoked meats.

SALT AND VINEGAR

Adding salt to food has a similar effect to smoking or drying. Bacteria and fungi on meat are dried out by salt and die. Salting only affects the surface of the meat. Inside, it remains juicy.

Before modern forms of food preservation were invented, salt used for pickling was a valuable commodity. Salt occurs in the ground. Digging it out is still an important business. Salt pans are shallow pools where salty water evaporates in the heat of the Sun. Dry salt crystals are left behind. The sea salt sold in stores is made by filling salt pans with seawater.

A liquid equivalent of salting is to store food in brine (salted water). Olives and fish are often preserved in this way. Pickling uses vinegar or alcohol to keep food from spoiling. Vinegar is a dilute acid. Alcohol and vinegar kill most bacteria. Pickled food can last for months or years, although the process alters flavors strongly. (*Continued on page 65.*)

Pickling vegetables in vinegar is one way of preserving them for a long time. Most types of bacteria that would ordinarily damage the food cannot survive in the acid vinegar. People pickle food in summer so it keeps until winter.

All meat produced in a slaughterhouse must be inspected for diseases. The inspectors are looking for signs that the animal was diseased or infected with parasites, such as worms.

The journey livestock makes from the fields to the butcher's shop is one that few people think about. Even so, it is an important part of food production and employs many people.

Most livestock is raised with a view to slaughter. Even cattle kept for milking end up eventually as meat. Farm animals raised specifically for meat are slaughtered as soon as they reach the right size. For farmers, there is no point in feeding livestock for any longer than is absolutely necessary. Animal feed costs money, and a quick turnover means greater profit. Cattle raised for meat are usually slaughtered at around one year of age, pigs and sheep at three to eight months, and chickens at five or six weeks.

Livestock is killed for meat in slaughterhouses. Animals are sold at markets by farmers and then taken straight to a slaughterhouse in modified trucks. The trucks have roofs but have vents in the side that let in air. Once at the slaughterhouse the animals are off-loaded into large holding pens. They are kept there until the slaughterer is ready to deal with them. Cattle, sheep, and pigs are driven into individual holding pens to prevent them from moving about. They are rendered unconscious before having their throats cut. The stunning is carried out using gas, an electric shock, or a bolt through the brain.

Chickens are killed in a different way. The birds are shackled upside-down by their feet and hooked to a moving line, which looks something like a conveyor belt. The line passes over an electrified water bath. Dipping the chickens' heads in the electrified water stuns or kills the birds before the line takes them to an automatic neck cutter.

After slaughter, most farm animals have their skins cut off and are butchered. Cow and pig skins are used for leather to make shoes and clothing. Sheepskins are made into coats or rugs for the home. Butchering involves cutting the flesh into joints, many of which have particular names. Loin is taken from the lower half of the animal's back, chuck from the shoulder, and shank from the leg. Other cuts include flank and short plate, both taken from the belly. Not all

> *Once animals arrive at a slaughterhouse, they are kept in large pens and given plenty of food. This keeps them calm and contented before being killed.*

meat is sold as joints. Little of an animal's carcass is wasted. Even after all the joints are removed the bones are blasted with water or soaked in solvents to remove any remaining meat. Much of it is processed into products such as burgers (below). Sausages are made by squeezing minced meat mixed with other products into a synthetic skin. People once used animal intestines for sausage skins. Now most skins are formed from regenerated cellulose film, which is manufactured from wood or cotton.

Meat processing and packing is an enormous industry. The people of the United States eat an estimated more than 50 billion burgers a year. Fast-food products such as burgers are made in huge factories that employ thousands of people. Each production-line patty probably contains meat from dozens of different animals.

Refrigeration

Keeping food cold is one of the best ways of preserving it because chilling does not alter the flavor of the food. Ice chillers were first used thousands of years ago. In Mesopotamia meat was kept in pits filled with ice as long ago as 2000 B.C.E. The Greeks and Romans also maintained ice pits covered with straw to keep things cold in the summer.

The domestic refrigerator was not invented until around 1850. The first models appeared in the United States. They were slate-lined wooden boxes, well insulated and built to contain blocks of ice. The ice was cut from frozen rivers in the winter and stored until needed. By 1856, refrigerators with a separate ice compartment were being made.

The first mechanical domestic refrigerator was invented in 1879 by the German engineer Karl von Linde. It kept things cool by the repeated compression and evaporation of ammonia, achieved using a steam-powered pump. In 1923 the electric refrigerator was introduced by two Swedish engineers, Carl Munters and Balzer von Platen. They sold the patents for their design to Chicago's Kelvinator company in 1925.

Poisonous coolants, such as ammonia and sulfuric acid, were replaced in the 1930s with a new substance called Freon. Freon is a chlorofluorocarbon (CFC). It was used in refrigerators in developed countries until the 1990s and is still used in some developing countries. CFCs are now known to damage the ozone layer in the atmosphere. Alternative coolants such as hydrofluorocarbons and isobutane are thought to be less harmful and are now used in place of freon.

5
4
3
2
1

1. A pump compresses the coolant so it becomes a hot, high-pressure liquid.

2. The liquid flows through long coiled condenser pipes where it releases heat into the air behind the refrigerator.

3. The liquid is squirted through a nozzle. It expands very rapidly becoming a cold gas.

4. The cold gas coolant passes through more coiled pipes called an evaporator.

5. The air inside the refrigerator compartment warms the coolant gas and becomes colder itself. The coolant returns to the compressor.

This can of food was taken on an expedition to the Arctic by British explorer Edward Perry in 1823. It was not used during that journey, and the can remained sealed until 1939. Then it was opened to confirm that its contents were still fresh.

Like vinegar, spices change the way food tastes. In the past they were used both to preserve foods and to mask bad flavors of food that had started to rot. Spices became very valuable. Nations grew rich on the trade. The search for spices even started empires.

OTHER METHODS

One way to keep food fresh and retain its flavor is to cool or freeze it. People often think of the icebox as a recent invention but this preservation technique has a very long history. In the past people collected ice on high mountains. Now ice is made in refrigerators. Synthetic coolants are pumped through pipes on the back of the refrigerator. The pressure turns the coolants into liquids, and they release heat into the air. Inside the appliance, the gas is released through a nozzle into wider pipes. The gas expands rapidly, and its pressure and temperature drop rapidly. Warm air inside the refrigerator transfers heat to the cooled refrigerant gas, lowering the temperature inside.

Many new methods of food preservation have appeared since the beginning of the industrial Revolution. In 1795, the French chef Nicolas Appert took jars of food sealed with cork and placed them in boiling water. He found that the food inside stayed fresh for much longer than it would have done otherwise. Appert entered his discovery into a competition organized by the French government and won. He used the prize money to perfect his system and set himself up in business. Appert's system worked because the heat from the boiling water killed off bacteria in the jar. The cork seal prevented fresh bacteria getting in. Appert never knew why his process worked because bacteria were not discovered until after his death.

Appert's system was taken a step farther in 1810, when another Frenchman, Pierre Durand, invented a metal container for preserving food. Durand's patent was bought the following year by John Hall

Pasteurization

Today we take safe milk for granted but before Louis Pasteur (1822–95; above) it was anything but safe. Pasteur was a 19th-century French scientist. In 1856 he was asked by wine producers to find out why some their wine had been turning sour. What he discovered was that there were two types of yeast in the wine. One produced alcohol, as expected, but the other later began making acid, which spoiled the wine. Pasteur's advice was to heat the wine gently after it had been made. This would kill the yeast after the alcohol had already been made but before the acid spoiled the wine. Pasteur applied the process to milk in 1862. Before that time, milk sold to the public had often harbored dangerous microorganisms, including those responsible for tuberculosis. Pasteur's heat treatment, now named pasteurization, killed the microorganisms and made milk safe to drink. Pasteurization became a widely used technique. It is applied to many different sorts of foodstuffs, including fruit juice and fish.

 Fact Ultrahigh temperature (UHT) treatments heat milk to 280° F (138° C) for a few seconds. UHT milk does not have to be refrigerated and stays fresh for three months.

and Brian Donkin, two industrialists from England. They went on to sell the first mass-produced canned foods. They used tin to line their handmade iron cans, which had to be broken into with a hammer and spike. The first can opener was invented in 1855. Tin-free steel cans like those we use today first appeared in 1965.

PRESERVATIVES

Many processed foods contain artificial preservatives. Some of these chemicals are antimicrobial agents, killing bacteria that would otherwise cause the food to spoil. Sodium nitrate and sorbic acid are among the most commonly used preservatives of this kind. Other substances, called antioxidants, help prevent changes in color, texture, or flavor when food is exposed to air. People have been adding artificial preservatives to food since the 19th century, although their use is now much more widespread.

The most modern method of food preservation is irradiation. Although patented as long ago as 1905, it has only been used widely since the 1960s. Irradiation is especially useful for prolonging the shelf life of fruit, vegetables, and raw meat. Irradiated food does not have to be heated and so the process is good for preserving raw goods. Bacteria is killed off by exposure to gamma radiation. The food does not become radioactive during the irradiation process.

FOOD PREPARATION

People have cooked food ever since they first harnessed fire. Cooking destroys dangerous microorganisms, which are killed by the heat. Long before they realized this, people cooked food to improve the taste and make it easier to chew and swallow.

People around the world have developed all sorts of different ways of cooking. Some methods, such as boiling and steaming, use water. Others, such as frying, require the addition of fat. The implements that go with these processes are familiar to all of us. Apart from using new materials, such as pyrex and nonstick Teflon, cooking tools have changed little in hundreds of years.

One area that has changed over the years is the design of ovens.

Where once people cooked over an open fire fueled with wood or coal, now we have gas, electricity, and microwaves. Cooking has become much less of a chore than it once was. Thermostats and timers make the process more precise and we start and stop the heat with the flick of a switch.

The Microwave Oven

How things work

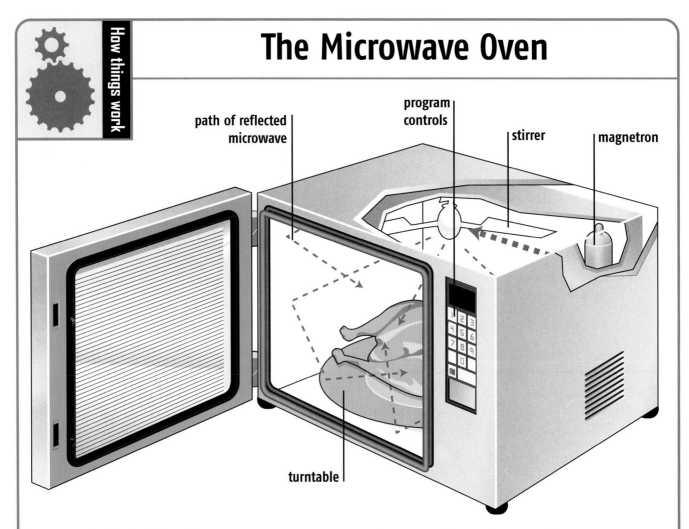

path of reflected microwave

program controls

stirrer

magnetron

turntable

Most people think of the microwave oven as a recent invention but it dates back to 1953. The first model was patented by the Raytheon Manufacturing Company of Massachusetts under the title High-Frequency Dialectric Heating Apparatus. It was sold mostly to the catering trade, where it was used to heat many precooked meals at once. Smaller versions began appearing in homes in the late 1960s.

Microwaves themselves were first produced in 1940 by physicists at Birmingham University in England. The microwave radiation is produced by a machine called a magnetron. Microwaves were being used in radars, but it was soon found that they also caused molecules inside substances to vibrate making heat. When applied to food, the waves vibrate the water and fat molecules so much that the food cooks from the inside.

Margarine is perhaps the most widely used artificial food. It is made from liquid vegetable oils, which are treated to become more solid like butter. Many people prefer to eat and cook with margarine because it has less fat than butter.

MAKING NEW FOODS

Creating dishes by adding ingredients together is an age-old practice. Making foods not found in nature is a relatively new practice. Wine, cheese, and yogurt are all made by adding microorganisms, but these are exceptions. Most artificial foods came into existence in the last couple of centuries.

One of the first mass-produced synthetic foodstuffs was margarine. Margarine was invented as a result of a competition launched by French emperor and soldier Napoleon Bonaparte (1769–1821) to find an alternative to butter. Its creator, the French chemist Hippolyte Mège-Mouriès, made his margarine from animal fats. In 1902, a German called Wilhelm Normann greatly altered and improved the recipe when he discovered that vegetable oils exposed to hydrogen gas produced solid fats. Today, hydrogenated vegetable oil is used.

Margarine was soon followed by saccharine, the first artificial sweetener. Saccharine was discovered in 1879 by the U.S. scientist Constantin Fahlberg. It quickly became an extremely successful substitute for sugar. Unlike sugar, saccharine has virtually no calories, making it very popular with people who are trying to lose weight. Also, saccharine does not cause teeth to rot as sugar does. Health concerns linked to saccharine have led to it being largely replaced by aspartame, or Nutrasweet. This sweetener was discovered in 1965 by American scientists at the Searle Laboratory. Like saccharine, aspartame is many times sweeter than sugar but has almost no calories.

Other new foods made in the 20th century include two types of meat substitute. Textured vegetable protein, made from soy beans, was invented by U.S. chemist Robert Boyer in 1953. It was joined in 1989 by mycoprotein, a meat substitute made from strands of fungus protein.

Sugar Production

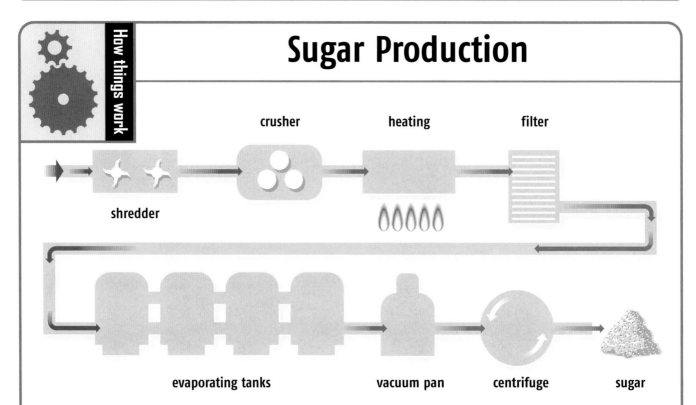

crusher   heating   filter

shredder

evaporating tanks   vacuum pan   centrifuge   sugar

Like salt and spices, sugar is a substance we tend to add to food instead of eat on its own. People eat vast quantities of sugar, more than 120 million tons (108 metric tons) a year globally. It is produced in many parts of the world from one of two sources, sugar beet or sugar cane. Sugar beet has the advantage that it can be grown almost anywhere. Sugar cane only grows in the warm tropics. A type of huge grass, cane can reach 15 feet (5 m) tall and yields much more sugar than beets.

Sugar reaches its familiar white crystal form by a complex process. In the case of sugar cane (above), the sweet juice must first be extracted by crushing the harvested grass. Once extracted, the juice is cleaned of dirt by adding a chemical called calcium hydroxide (slaked lime). Next, the juice is thickened into a syrup by boiling. The boiling continues until most of the water has been evaporated off, and crystals have started to grow.

The resulting mixture is dried in a partial vacuum and then spun in a centrifuge to separate the crystals from the last of the syrup. At this stage the syrup is known as molasses. The sugar crystals are sticky and brown.

Changing them into white sugar is called refining. Most often the refining takes place in the country where the sugar is sold. In refining, raw brown sugar is dissolved into a concentrated syrup. This is treated with chalk and later granulated carbon to remove color and impurities. Once the syrup has become clear, it is boiled. White sugar crystals form and are removed from the liquid by spinning. Making white sugar from sugar beet is less complicated. First, the beets are sliced into chips. The chips are crushed to extract the juice. The juice is boiled to evaporate off water and begin crystal formation. Finally, the solution is spun to separate out the white crystals for packing.

COFFEE AND COLA

It is not just solid foods that have changed since the Industrial Revolution began. Drinks have also altered and many entirely new beverages have been invented. A key development in drink production was the introduction of carbonation, which makes water fizzy. Carbonation is achieved by running cold water over metal plates in a sealed tank of carbon dioxide. The tank is kept under high pressure, which forces some of the gas to dissolve into the water, making a very weak acid.

One of the first people to market carbonated water was the Swiss chemist Jacob Schweppe. His new drink went on sale in 1794. Before long, fizzy drinks could be bought in a variety of flavors. In 1886 John Pemberton of Atlanta, Georgia, invented Coca-Cola, now one of the world's most recognized brand names. The recipe included stimulants from the coca plant and cola nuts, which were replaced later with caffeine.

Almost as important to the drinks industry as carbonation was the invention of instant coffee. Powdered instant coffee was first produced by the Japanese chemist Satori Kato. He introduced his creation to the world at the Pan American Exposition in 1901. Powdered coffee is made from very strong coffee extract, which is sprayed through a jet of hot air to evaporate off the water.

In 1906 two French chemists, Arsene d'Arsonval and F. Bordas, made the first freeze-dried instant coffee. Freeze-drying causes substances to dry out by exposing them to a sudden and extreme drop in pressure.

Instant coffee is made by freeze-drying a strong brew of coffee made from fresh beans (left). Adding hot water to the instant coffee powder (right) will turn it back into a piping-hot drink.

71

STOVES

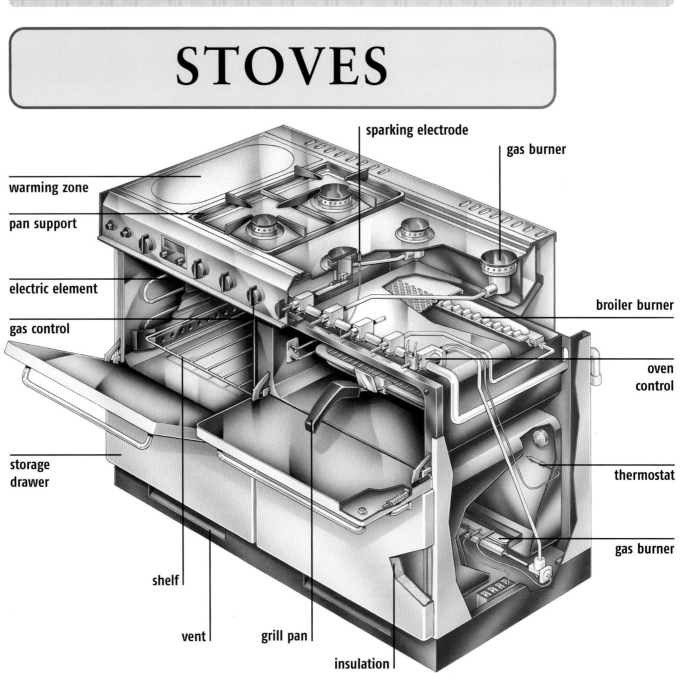

sparking electrode

gas burner

warming zone

pan support

electric element

gas control

broiler burner

oven control

storage drawer

thermostat

gas burner

shelf

vent

grill pan

insulation

Cooking food makes it easier to digest. It also makes it safer, killing bacteria and destroying any parasites before they enter our bodies. People cooked their food over open fires for thousands of years. In some places people still cook in this way. The first ovens appeared more than 3,000 years ago. Simple vessels of clay or dried mud,

they were heated by lighting a fire inside. When the oven was hot, the fire and ashes were swept out and the food to be cooked put in. Smaller ovens were heated by placing them in front of fires. Even when metal replaced clay the design remained simple.

The first true stoves were introduced in the 17th century. A stove is a free-standing,

closed device that burns fuel internally to cook food or generate heat. Ranges were also used for heating as well as cooking. They had an open fire which fed a metal oven and a cooktop for heating pots. The stove developed from the range. The earliest stoves were used by settlers in North America, cast in Pennsylvania iron foundries.

Until the 1920s, most Americans cooked on wood-burning stoves. During this decade gas and electric stoves became more widely available.

Most stoves today are powered by gas or electricity. The first person to cook with gas was Zuchas Winzler, a chemical manufacturer from Moravia (today called the Czech Republic). From 1802, Winzler gave dinner parties in his home, serving dishes cooked on a gas stove of his own design. Similar experiments followed but the first real breakthrough came in 1855 when the German scientist Robert Wilhelm von Bunsen invented his now famous burner. The Bunsen burner mixed gas with air before it burned so it made much hotter flames. The first gas ovens to go on sale used this technology.

Cooking with electricity became widespread a little later than gas. The first electric oven was powered by a generator driven by a nearby waterfall. This oven was installed in the Hotel Bernina near St. Moritz, Switzerland, in 1889. Domestic electric stoves began appearing in homes in the 1920s. Early models were crude and had no thermostat (temperature control). The first electric oven with temperature control was produced in 1933.

The heat generated by electric stoves is produced by passing an electric current through coiled wire. The wire gets hot and heats a hollow metal sheath, or element. The element transfers heat to the pan. Some electric cookers have hobs with spiral-shaped elements. In others, the element is concealed beneath a heat-conducting plate. The cooktop may be made of one of several different materials. Many are metal but others are ceramic or glasslike. Halogen cooktops are heat pans that use a very hot light.

Modern stoves have many energy-saving features. Doors are insulated to minimize heat loss. Timers alert the user or control the oven.

Ceramic cooktops use an electrical element to heat a glasslike plate that heats pans.

Halogen cooktops heat pans using a strong heat-giving lamp.

Induction cooktops use a magnetic field from an electric coil to heat pans without having to heat an element.

TRADITIONAL CLOTHING

A few animals cover themselves to hide from enemies, but people are the only animals to make and wear clothes. Clothes have two main functions: To keep us warm and to change our appearance.

The first clothes were the skins, or hides, of animals killed by hunters for food. The flesh was removed using stone scrapers and the skins were wrapped around the body for warmth. Around 40,000 years ago, people began joining pieces of skins, using sinew or thongs made from strips of hide. Bone needles dating from this period have been discovered, as have decorative items such as rings and beads. Even 40,000 years ago, people were wearing items for decoration as well as for comfort. More recent cultures have used animal skins as camouflage to help them get closer to prey while hunting. We cannot be certain, but it seems likely that prehistoric people also used skins for this purpose.

ANIMAL FIBERS

Animal skins are still used for clothing today. Leather is hide that has been treated with tannin, a yellow liquid extracted from boiling bark. Tannin makes leather more waterproof and durable in cold weather.

Most leather used for shoes, belts, or jackets starts out as raw cow hide or pig skin. Other animals that provide leather include kangaroos, crocodiles, and snakes. Sheepskin is sheep hide with the fur still attached.

When fur is removed from sheep or goats, it can be twisted and rolled to make wool. Wool was one of the first fibers people used to make fabric. Archaeological evidence suggests that people in Mesopotamia were wearing woolen clothes 10,000 years ago. Once rolled into yarn, wool was woven—a technique already familiar to basketmakers—to create sheets of fabric that could be made into garments. Wool is warmer, lighter, and more flexible

Key inventions

Natural Rubber

Rubber has been known to South American peoples for centuries. It is made from latex, the milky sap of rubber trees. The sap is collected (above) by slicing into the tree's bark. The liquid drips into containers strapped to the trunk. Rubber trees grow wild in the rain forests of Brazil. Since the 1870s, rubber has been cultivated in various tropical countries around the world. Natural rubber was first used in clothing by Charles Macintosh. In 1823 he added rubber to cotton to make waterproof fabric.

Spinning a Yarn

distaff

spindle

wheel

pedal

To turn wool or cotton into cloth it must first be spun into yarn, or thread. Most natural fibers are just a few inches long. They are more or less useless for weaving unless twisted together to make a longer, stronger thread. The first people to make yarn rolled individual wool fibers together between their hands. Cotton and linen yarns were also made in this way. By 7000 B.C.E. people were using the distaff and spindle. Fibers drawn out from a stick, the distaff, were hooked in a notch at the top of another stick, the spindle. The spindle was weighted at the end with a round stone.

The operator, or spinster, span the spindle, twisting the fibers together into a tight yarn. The spinning wheel probably originated in India. In the early 14th century it appeared in Europe. The function of the spinning wheel was simply to rotate the spindle mechanically. The first models were turned by hand with the spinster still holding a separate distaff. In the 15th century the entire device was transformed. Wheel, distaff, and spindle were all incorporated into a single machine (left). The wheel was spun by a foot pedal, which moved up and down. This left the spinster's hands free to do other work.

than leather. The Incas of South America used the fleece of alpacas for weaving. Most modern woollen clothes are knitted, either by hand or machine. The exact origin of knitting is a mystery. Some experts claim it originated in the Middle East, others think it started in North Africa. The oldest known knitted objects are socks from Egyptian tombs dated between the 3rd and 6th centuries B.C.E.

Wool is not the only animal fiber used to make clothes. Silk has been farmed in China for more than 4,000 years. Silk is created by an insect, the caterpillar of a large moth. Like wool, the raw silk fiber is twisted to make thread before it is woven into fabric. Silk is smooth to the touch and has long been a highly prized material. Trade in silk joined continents. People transported it across mountains and deserts from China to the Mediterranean and the Roman Empire.

PLANT FIBERS AND DYES

After woven wool, the second most ancient fabric is probably linen. As long ago as 3,400 B.C.E. Egyptian mummies were wrapped in linen. The cloth is made from

Silk worms, the caterpillars of a large moth, spin silk threads to make their cocoons. People in China were the first to use these fine threads to make luxury cloth.

Cotton fibers are harvested from the seed heads of the cotton plant.

fibers in the stem of the flax plant. This slender plant also yields linseed oil. Flax is grown in many parts of the world.

Not long after people began making linen, cotton was first used for clothing in India. By 2000 B.C.E. people were also making cotton fabrics in Peru. Cotton fibers grow attached to the seeds of the cotton plant. For centuries, the job of separating the fibers from the seeds was done by hand. In 1793, an American called Eli Whitney (1765–1825) invented the cotton gin. Whitney's machine worked by pulling the cotton through spinning blades. The fibers passed through but the seeds were left behind. The device sped up the cotton cleaning process so much that within a few years of its introduction the slave-driven United States textile industry was producing 50 times more cotton than it had before.

Today, cotton is the most widely used natural fiber. Like flax, silk, and most wool, cotton is whitish when produced. The cotton garments most of us wear are colored by dyes. Nowadays we have many synthetic dyes. Before the 1850s, all dyes were natural

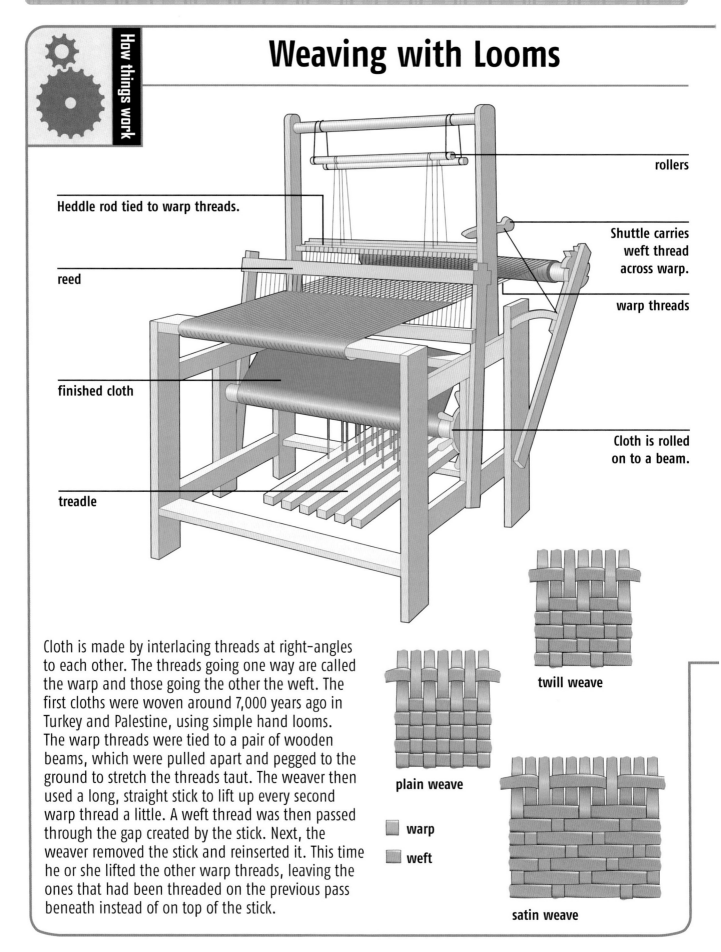

Weaving with Looms

rollers

Heddle rod tied to warp threads.

Shuttle carries weft thread across warp.

reed

warp threads

finished cloth

Cloth is rolled on to a beam.

treadle

twill weave

plain weave

satin weave

warp

weft

Cloth is made by interlacing threads at right-angles to each other. The threads going one way are called the warp and those going the other the weft. The first cloths were woven around 7,000 years ago in Turkey and Palestine, using simple hand looms. The warp threads were tied to a pair of wooden beams, which were pulled apart and pegged to the ground to stretch the threads taut. The weaver then used a long, straight stick to lift up every second warp thread a little. A weft thread was then passed through the gap created by the stick. Next, the weaver removed the stick and reinserted it. This time he or she lifted the other warp threads, leaving the ones that had been threaded on the previous pass beneath instead of on top of the stick.

Hand looms were in use for 2,000 years. Then, around 3000 B.C.E., warp-weighted looms were invented. Instead of being tied to two beams, the warp threads were hung over a single crossbar and held taut by weights tied to their ends. In around 1400 B.C.E. two-bar vertical looms followed, with the warp threads strung to cross-bars. This type of loom is still used to weave tapestry today.

As time passed the hand loom became ever more intricate (left). First it was attached to a rigid frame, then heddle rods were invented. Heddle rods were suspended over the now horizontal body of the loom and attached by strings to every second warp thread. When a heddle rod was lifted, it would create the gap that in primitive hand looms had been made by inserting a stick. By using two heddle rods suspended from a roller, the warp threads could be lifted alternately in quick succession. In the Middle Ages a foot pedal, or treadle, was added to make moving the heddles easier. A device called a reed enabled the weaver to pull the weft threads tightly into place.

A loom invented by Frenchman Joseph Marie Jacquard in 1801 used punched cards as guides for weaving complex patterns in cloth. The loom's cards are thought to be the first software programs.

products. Perhaps the oldest is indigo, a plant dye. It has been used since at least 3000 B.C.E. Clothes colored with indigo have been discovered at sites dating back to the time of the first pharaohs in ancient Egypt. Farther north, blue dye was obtained from the leaves of the woad plant. The purple togas of Roman emperors were colored with a dye from a sea snail. Red dye was extracted from the roots of the madder plant or from the safflower, which resembles a thistle. All of the ancient dyes needed to be fixed using a fixative chemical, or mordant. These stopped colors from running, or washing out of the cloth. Mordants varied from tannin to solutions of metals such as tin. The scarcity of their ingredients often made dyed clothes expensive and desirable.

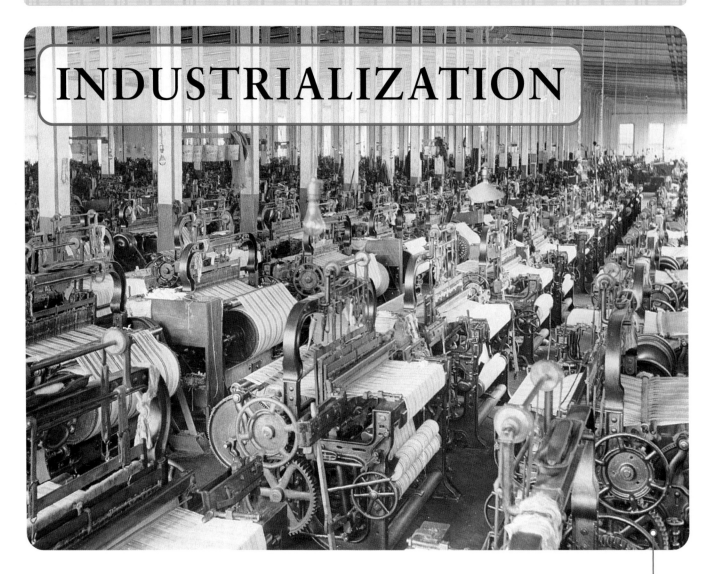

INDUSTRIALIZATION

Peoples' working patterns began to change in the 1700s. Many jobs that had been done by hand became mechanized. In 1701, Jethro Tull invented the mechanical seed drill. Within decades, the revolution spread to the clothing industry.

In 1733, the English weaver John Kay invented a device called the flying shuttle. It changed forever the way cloth was made. Before Kay, weavers had built up sheets of cloth slowly, hand-drawing individual weft threads through lines of separated warp threads. The flying shuttle mechanized this action, enabling cloth to be made much more quickly. Because the weaver no longer had to reach through the warp threads, the flying shuttle also allowed cloth to be made wider.

The invention of the flying shuttle made looms much more efficient. Weavers were suddenly able to produce far more cloth than before. Increased output led to a rise in the demand for thread. In

Textile mills were the first factories. Workers used mechanized looms that produced huge quantities of wool and cotton fabric.

1767 an Englishman called James Hargreaves came up with a device to meet that demand. His invention, the spinning jenny, could spin eight different threads at once and was operated by a single person. The yarn it produced was soft and suitable only for the weft threads. The spinning jenny took a lot of pressure off spinners, who were struggling to produce thread fast enough to feed the rapidly growing market. Two years later another Englishman, Richard Arkwright, mechanized spinning further. His water frame was driven by a belt attached to a water wheel. It produced thread strong enough for both warp and weft threads.

OPENING THE MILLS

Spinning and weaving were cottage industries. Yarn and cloth were made by craftspeople working from their own homes. Richard Arkwright brought that tradition to an end when he built his first textile mill. Arkwright's mill opened in 1771. It changed more than just the way people worked, it also changed how they lived. People began traveling to start work at a particular time; Arkwright's employees were the forerunners of today's commuters. As more factories were built, new communities grew up in specially built industrial towns. The old country ways declined as the population became urbanized. The farmers left behind in the countryside now produced food for the people who had once grown their own.

Arkwright's textile mill was powered by water. In 1790 a similar mill for spinning cotton was built beside the Blackstone River on Rhode Island. These early factories were noisy but at least they were clean. That all changed with the introduction of machinery powered by steam engines. By 1797 water-driven factories were being superceded by factories that burned coal to boil water for

In the early days of industry, children were put to work. In the 1830s nearly half of all factory workers in New England were under 12.

steam. The new factories had tall chimneys that pumped out great clouds of smoke.

The textile industry underwent another major change in the early 1800s with the introduction of the Jacquard loom. Designed in 1801 by its French namesake, Joseph Marie Jacquard, this loom is still used for making elaborate fabrics. It uses perforated cards to guide hooks to lift particular warp threads. Different cards produce cloth with different patterns. The Jacquard loom was a milestone in the history of automation. The cards are the first examples of computer software.

MODERN MATERIALS

Natural fibers have their limits. Cotton and linen garments come out of the wash wrinkled, silk requires delicate handling, and woolen garments shrink in hot water. Clothing manufacturers long dreamed of producing fibers that had none of these problems. It was the 19th century before this dream started to come true.

ARTIFICIAL FIBERS
The first patent for an artificial fiber was granted in England in 1855. A Swiss chemist named Georges Audemars had created what he dubbed "artificial silk" from cellulose, a substance found in plants. Audemars obtained his raw product by dissolving the inner bark of the mulberry tree in

Many cyclists wear synthetic materials. Cycle gear is tight to minimize wind resistance. The fabrics also take moisture from the skin and release it into the air.

a chemical solution. He created threads by dipping a needle in the cellulose and slowly removing it to draw the fibers out.

Despite it being easier to use than real silk, Audemars' invention never became popular. In the early 1880s the English chemist and electrician Joseph Swan tried to revive artificial silk by inventing a new production method. Instead of drawing fibers out with a needle, Swan created threads by forcing the cellulose through tiny holes. In 1885 his wife used the fibers to crochet a fabric, which he exhibited in London. Swan's other area of expertise was electric lightbulbs. His success in the field of

Key inventions

Holding It Together

For almost as long as there have been clothes, there have been clothes fasteners. Even before people made fabrics, they made pins of bone or antler to hold together animal hides. The most ancient fasteners that we might recognize today are brooches and buttons. The Celts of northern Europe used brooches to pin their coats and dresses at the shoulder. Buttons have an equally long history. Toggles connected to string loops were in use in the Middle East 4,000 years ago. The Romans used buttons almost identical to the modern version. Roman buttons were sewn to cloth and designed to pass through a slit. The first hook fasteners were used in medieval England. In 1891, the zipper was invented by American Whitcomb Judson. Judson's zipper had hooks and eyes that locked together by pulling a slide. In 1906 a Swedish engineer called Gideon Sundback improved on Judson's design. His zipper had interlocking metal teeth and resembled the zippers we use today (left).

The most recent development of clothes fasteners was the invention of Velcro in 1948. Velcro was the brainchild of a Swiss engineer called George de Mestral, who was inspired by the way seeds from the burdock plant gripped onto clothes while out hiking. The seeds have hundreds of hooks that stick on clothes, fur, or feathers. Back in the office, de Mestral designed a strip of nylon with hooks. He then made another strip covered in loops for the tiny hooks to grip on to.

Washing Machines

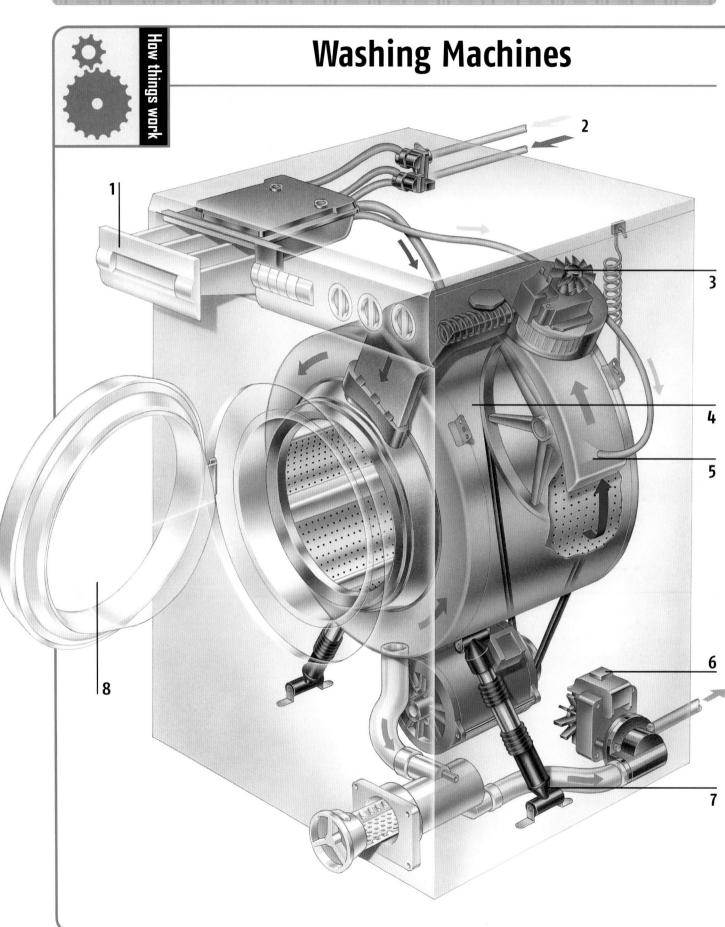

1

2

3

4

5

6

7

8

Until recent times, doing the laundry was a time consuming chore. Clothes were scrubbed by hand or rubbed with soap on a ridged washboard. Clothes were dried by hanging them out in the sun after squeezing them through a mangle—two rollers, one turned by hand, the other held in a metal frame.

Today we have machines that do all of the heavy work. The first washing machine was invented in 1782 by Henry Sidgier, a London upholsterer. The machine comprised a cylindrical cage of wooden rods held inside a hexagonal barrel. The cage contained the clothes and was turned by hand using a crank handle.

The first electric washing machine appeared in 1906. Designed by Alva Fisher of Chicago, it had a motor to rotate its horizontal drum. In 1926, New York's Savage Arms Corporation built the first combined washer and spin drier. The clothes were washed in a drum held at a 45° angle. In order to dry the clothes, the drum had to be lifted off and placed on a vertical drive shaft. This spun much more quickly to force out the water.

Electric water heaters and pumps were added to washing machines in the late 1940s. A few years later tumble dryers were invented that blew hot air through a revolving drum. Today, we have fully automatic machines that soak, wash, rinse, spin, and dry. The cycles are controlled by electric sensors and time switches, which monitor both water temperature and the drum spin speed.

Front-Loading Washer-Drier

Some washing machines are loaded through a door in their tops. They spin clothes using rotating paddles inside. Front-loading models use less water and spin the clothes in a drum. Washer-driers use hot air to dry washed clothes.

1. Detergent powder or liquid is added to this drawer before washing begins.

2. Hot and cold water are drawn into the machine during washing.

3. A heater warms the air used to dry the clothes.

4. The clothes are placed in a steel drum for washing. The drum has many small holes in it to let dirty water flow out.

5. When the clothes are clean, hot air is blown through the drum. This hot, wet air is cooled by a spray of cold water. As it cools, the air releases moisture picked up from the wet clothes.

6. Moisture from the condenser or dirty water are pumped away.

7. Dampers keep the drum steady as it spins.

8. The plastic door is watertight.

electric lights caused him to put his work in fabrics on hold. Eventually he abandoned textiles.

A NEW MARKET
The first real breakthrough in synthetic fibers came at the Paris Exhibition in 1889. The French chemist Count Hilaire de Chardonnet showed his version of artificial silk at the exhibition. The count's exhibit caused a sensation and he was inspired to produce his fabrics commercially. Two years later, he opened his first factory and secured his place in history. He became known as the father of rayon. Rayon is the name now given to all forms of cellulose-based materials.

Rayon did not really break into the U.S. market for another 20 years. It was 1910 before Samuel Courtaulds and Co. formed the American Viscose Company and began commercial production of the now-famous material viscose. The demand for synthetic fibers grew and grew. Today, 70 percent of all fibers used in the United States are artificial.

THE NEXT BIG THING
After rayon came nylon, the best-known synthetic fiber of all. Nylon was created by the American scientist Wallace Carothers in 1931 while he was working in the laboratories of the DuPont Company. Nylon was patented in 1937 and improved in 1938 by a German chemist called Paul Schlack. The first nylon stockings,

Nylon's best-known use is for pantyhose. Nylons replaced silk hose, which were easily damaged.

Kevlar is a lightweight artificial fiber five times stronger than steel. It was invented in 1966 and is used to make bulletproof vests.

which were much stronger and durable than traditional silk ones, went on sale in 1940.

Nylon was revolutionary, not only because of its properties but also because of its source. It is made from crude oil. The new fabric inspired research into what would quickly become a whole new range of artificial materials made from petrochemicals.

A LONG STRETCH

Work with the new artificial fibers soon generated results. In 1959 the DuPont chemist Joseph Shivers created Spandex from polyurethane. The company subsequently branded another stretchy substance called Lycra. By the beginning of the 1960s people were finding uses for Lycra in pantyhose and underwear. Today Lycra is used in just about every type of figure-hugging garment imaginable, from sportswear to shoes.

Waterproofing

Key inventions

There are many different ways to make clothes waterproof. The easiest is to use water-resistant fabric. Natural waterproof materials are rare but do exist. Before the invention of synthetic materials, whale skin was one of the few leathers that could be used untreated. Other types of leather also repel water but must be treated to protected them from damage. Another way to waterproof fabric is to add a water-resistant substance to it. Cotton cloth may be waterproofed by rubbing in wax. The wax has to be reapplied regularly for the waterproofing to remain effective. A more permanent solution is to dip cloth in a durable water-resistant substance at manufacture. This is what Charles Macintosh first did with rubber in 1823. Synthetic waterproof fabrics are now regularly used in clothing. One of the most widespread waterproofing agents is Teflon, invented by Roy Plunkett in 1938. Teflon is the brand name for the massive molecule polytetrafluoroethene, which is a white, waxy solid. Teflon is so slippery that virtually nothing sticks to it, including oil. As well as being infused into fabrics for clothing, Teflon is used to coat nonstick frying pans.

 Fact **Waterproof rubber boots are often called "Wellington boots" after the 19th century British general and prime minister. Lord Wellington never used fully rubber boots, but in 1806 he asked for new leather boots covered with rubber.**

POLYMERS AND PLASTICS

The word *plastic* comes from ancient Greece. Originally the word meant molding or giving form to pliant matter. Today it has another, related meaning: Plastics are artificial substances that can be given any required shape.

Plastics are also known to scientists as synthetic polymers. A polymer is a giant chainlike molecule made up of many smaller parts called monomers. Not all polymers are synthetic. Some occur in nature. The stuff of hair and fingernails, collagen, is a natural polymer. So are lignin and cellulose, the principal components of wood.

The first synthetic plastic was a substance called parkesine. It was created in 1862 and named after its inventor, the English scientist Alexander Parkes. Parkesine was made by dissolving cellulose nitrate in a solvent. Like many other plastics that were to follow, parkesine could be molded and retained its shape when cooled. It was also transparent and by using dyes could be made any color. Unfortunately for Parkes, it was expensive to produce.

One of the next discoveries was celluloid, a brand name that is still familiar today. Celluloid was invented in

Plastic is the most versatile material ever invented. It can be made into everything from bags to pleasure boats. Plastics are polymers and are made from petroleum.

1869 by the American John Hyatt. It was envisioned as a replacement for ivory. At the time the game of billiards, which is similar to pool, was popular. The ivory used to make billiard balls was very expensive. Hyatt manufactured celluloid billiard balls. They turned out to have a serious flaw. The balls exploded when hit hard. Celluloid had many other applications. It was used eventually to make movie film and revolutionized the world of movies.

Before 1900, Parkesine and celluloid were two of just a handful of synthetic polymers. In the 20th century, they were joined by hundreds more. By the beginning of World War II (1939–45) polyethylene, plexiglas, and nylon had all been invented. After 1945 plastics became commonplace. Today it is hard to imagine life without them.

Plastics fall into one of two categories. Thermoplastics, such as celluloid, can be repeatedly softened and re-shaped. Thermosetting plastics, such as polyurethane, hold their shape when heated and cannot be re-softened.

All plastics are made by linking monomers together. The simplest polymers, called homopolymers, are chains of identical monomers. Polythene is a homopolymer made with molecules of ethylene, which occurs in natural gas. Ethylene gas is pressurized and heated to 300°F (150°C) in the presence of titanium and aluminum. The metals act as catalysts, modifying the ethylene molecules which then link to form a polymer chain. The long, straight chains of polyethylene pack tightly together, forming a dense plastic.

Other synthetic polymers have branched chains. These produce less dense plastics. By applying the right conditions, scientists can make bonds called crosslinks appear between polymer chains. Thermosetting plastics have large numbers of crosslink bonds that provide their rigid structure.

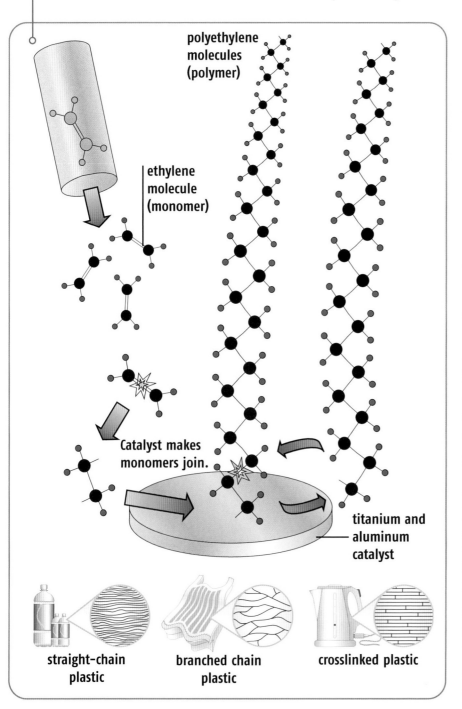

> *Polyethylene plastic is a chain of ethylene molecules. Polyethylene forms straight chains. More flexible plastics have branched chains, while plastics with crosslinked chains harden permanently and are used for devices that might get hot.*

polyethylene molecules (polymer)

ethylene molecule (monomer)

Catalyst makes monomers join.

titanium and aluminum catalyst

straight-chain plastic

branched chain plastic

crosslinked plastic

Time Line

1701
Jethro Tull develops his mechanized seed drill and the Agricultural Revolution begins.

16,000 B.C.E
The domestication of wheat begins in Egypt.

2000 B.C.E
Cattle are domesticated in Europe. Silk is being farmed in China.

1771
Richard Arkwright opens his textile mill. This is the world's first factory.

8000 B.C.E.
People keep pet dogs. Sheep and goats are domesticated in the Middle East. Woolen clothes first appear.

900 B.C.E.
Manure is first used as fertilizer in ancient Greece.

16,000 B.C.E.   2000 B.C.E.   1700 C.E.

1811
Mass-produced canned food appears.

3400 B.C.E.
The ancient Egyptians make the first linen fabrics.

1790s
Eli Whitney invents the cotton gin. Carbonated soft drinks go on sale.

1780
Artificial insemination is developed.

7500 B.C.E
The plow appears in Mesopotamia (modern Iraq).

1917
The Model F Fordson is introduced and tractors start to become widespread on farms.

1842
The first artificial fertilizers are manufactured.

1989
Mycoprotein meat substitutes go on sale.

1931
Nylon is created.

1850s
The domestic refrigerator is invented.

1940s
Artificial herbicides and pesticides are developed.

1860
Margarine is invented.

1840

1900

1990

1970s
Research into genetic engineering begins.

1906
Electric washing machine is invented.

1960s
Microwave ovens go on sale.

1891
The zipper is invented.

1959
Lycra, or spandex, is patented by DuPont.

1879
Saccharine is discovered.

2003
Genetically altered foods are available in the United States.

Glossary

aquaculture Farming animals or plants that live in water.

arable Farms that grow crops.

domestication The process of taking an animal or plant from the wild and taming it.

fertilizer A substance added to soil to make it more productive.

gene A section of DNA that codes for the production of a particular protein, or physical characteristic.

genetic engineering Altering the genes of an animal, plant or other living organism in the laboratory.

harpoon Spear used to kill whales.

herbicide A chemical that kills unwanted plants.

hydraulic Operated by means of fluid under pressure.

Industrial Revolution A period in the 19th centuries when the world adopted new technology moving from agricultural to industrial economies.

irradiation Preserving food by exposing it to radiation.

irrigation Supplying farm land with water.

livestock Animals bred and reared for farming.

medieval Relating to the Middle Ages, the period from around 1000 to 1500 c.e.

mollusk Animals such as squid, snails and shellfish.

nomad Someone who lives by moving from place to place.

organic farming Agriculture without the use of herbicides, pesticides or other artificial chemicals.

pastoral Associated with flocks or herds of livestock.

patent Authority from the government giving an individual or company the sole rights to produce an invention.

pesticide A chemical that kills insects and other crop pests.

prehistory The time before people made written records of events.

selective breeding Altering the way a plant or animal looks by breeding them from just a few chosen individuals.

subsistence hunter A person who hunts in order to survive.

thermostat A device that automatically regulates the temperature in a room.

transgenic Something that contains genetic material introduced from another species.

Further Resources

Books

Understanding Biotechnology by A. Borem, D. E. Bowen, and F. R. Santos. Prentice Hall PTR, 2003.

Farming and Food by J. Tarrant. Oxford University Press, 1991.

Fiber Science by S. B. Warner. Pearson Education, 1994.

Web Sites

About.com: Inventors

http://www.inventors.about.com/

Agropolis Museum

http://museum.agropolis.fr/english/default.htm

Smithsonian: Agriculture and Horticulture

http://www.si.edu/resource/faq/nmah/agriculture.htm

Index

Picture Credits